Abraham's Sandals of Faith

Prophetic Faith Keys to Life and Destiny

Crystal G.H. Lowery

© Copyright 2022 Crystal G. H. Lowery
All rights reserved.

No part of this publication may be reproduced or transmitted in any form or by any means, electronic or mechanical, including photocopying and recording, or by any information storage and retrieval system, except in the case of brief quotations for use in articles and reviews, without written permission from the author. The views expressed in this book are the author's and do not necessarily reflect those of the publisher.

www.WorldwidePublishingGroup.com
7710-T Cherry Park Dr, Ste 224
Houston, Texas 77095
(713) 766-4271

Cover photo by Teeography, www.Teeography.com
ISBN: xxxxxxxxxx

ENDORSEMENTS

Abraham's Sandals of Faith, by Crystal G.H. Lowery, is more than a book – it's like embarking on a journey with Abraham himself. The patriarch's life of faith and walk with God will challenge, convict and inspire you to believe God, according to His Word, against all odds!

-- **Daniel Kolenda**, President, *Christ for All Nations*

This is a profoundly rich and powerful book, encapsulating a message that will ignite within you the supernatural faith of Jesus. You will find as you journey through the pages, a fresh capacity to believe beginning to rise within your heart, sufficient to overcome any 'impossibility' you face. You will see with fresh eyes; inspired, empowered and knowing how to enter into this wonderful way of life.

-- **Liz Wright**, Founder *Liz Wright Ministries;* Podcast host of *Live Your Best Life with Liz Wright*, and international best-selling author of the book, *Reflecting God;* www.LizWright.org

The walk of faith is not always an easy journey. It's filled with risk, obstacles that need to be overcome and fears that must be faced along the way. In her book, ***Abraham's Sandals of Faith***, Crystal Lowery shares the astounding journey of Abraham, the father of faith and gives deep insight into how to experience the abundant life of overcoming faith. You will learn how to see impossibilities becoming possible and experience breakthrough in every area of your life. No matter how impossible the vision or promise of God to your heart, you can see if fully manifest, just as Abraham did. I encourage you to read and receive the supernatural faith that will be imparted to you through this wonderful book.

> **— Matt Sorger**, Prophetic Healing Minister; author of the book, *God's Unstoppable Breakthrough;* www.MattSorger.com

TABLE OF CONTENTS

FOREWORD .... **VII**
    THE PRICE OF YOUR FUTURE VIII

INTRODUCTION **1**

PART 1 .... **3**

CHAPTER 1 .... **4**

CHAPTER 1 .... **4**
    METHODS OF RECEIVING REVELATION AS A PROPHET 5
    ENCOUNTER #1 6
    ENCOUNTER #2 9
    SHECHEM 10
    OAK OF MOREH 12
    ENCOUNTER #3 15
    ENCOUNTER #4 17
    ENCOUNTER #5 22
    ENCOUNTER #6 33
    ENCOUNTER #7 46
    ENCOUNTER #8 (WITH SARAH) 58
    ENCOUNTER #9 63
    ENCOUNTER #10 68

PART 2 .... **79**

CHAPTER 2 .... **80**

CHAPTER 2 .... **80**

CHAPTER 3 .... **84**

CHAPTER 3 .... **84**
    MY SUCCESS WITH THIS PRINCIPLE: 88

CHAPTER 4 .... **97**

CHAPTER 4 .... **97**

CHAPTER 5 .... **114**

CHAPTER 5 .... **114**

    The Egypt Experience as Half-Siblings..*114*
    THE GERAR EXPERIENCE AS HALF-SIBLIINGS.................................... 124
    GERAR, THE SEQUEL WITH ISAAC AND REBEKAH................................ 129

CHAPTER 6 .... **134**

CHAPTER 6 .... **134**

CHAPTER 7 .... **148**

CHAPTER 7 .... **148**

CHAPTER 8 .... **163**

CHAPTER 8 .... **163**

CHAPTER 9 .... **178**

CHAPTER 9 .... **178**

CHAPTER 10 .... **195**

CHAPTER 1 0 .... **195**

CHAPTER 11 .... **214**

CHAPTER 11 .... **214**

REFERENCES **235**

FOREWORD

When I started reading this book, I was struck by this one simple theme: Trust is a big deal to God. The Jews know that because one of their repentance prayers during Rosh Hashanah is "forgive us for breach of trust." Breach means "broken" or "failure" and it's a serious offense.

As you walk through the pages of "Abraham's Sandals," you need to know Proverbs 3 and you need to meditate and pray about it. You need to have encounters with God and visit with Him through every single line, especially this one.

> "Trust in the Lord with all thine heart; and lean not unto thine own understanding." – Proverbs 3:5

This verse is crazy because this isn't how the world lives. You and I are called to live by faith, not according to our understanding. Your understanding is a result of your history. Trusting is knowing that what God Almighty is doing within your heart is considered your destiny.

Consider Abraham, a rock star of faith. He did not lean on his own understanding even though his body and Sarah, his wife, were well past the years of childbearing. But God promised Abraham a son through whom all the nations for the world would be blessed. For that, Abraham needed a lot of trust.

> "He did not waver at the promise of God through unbelief, but was strengthen in faith, giving glory to God, and being fully convinced that what He had promised He was also able to perform."
> – Romans 4:20-21

God has a destiny for each one of us. We need to find it and walk it out because legacy is the upgrade of destiny. King Jesus wants you to find your destiny so the legacy you leave will not be greatly diminished.

It's not about you. It's about how you glorify the Lord. You're supposed to be a fountain, right? You're supposed to be a well springing up. It's all about how you splash the Kingdom onto everything else.

We will all leave a legacy and hopefully one built of faith. A trust in God and in His word that says, "I know Him." A faith like Abraham's that glorifies God with all our heart. Faith that trusts in the goodness of God above everything else – a faith that has encountered God. That's rockstar faith and let me tell you, Abraham was a faith junkie.

The Price of Your Future

> Now the Lord had said to Abram: "Get out of your country, from your family, and from your father's house, to a land that I will show you. I will make you a great nation; I will bless you and make your name great; And you shall be a blessing. I will bless those who bless you, and I will curse him who curses you; And in you all the families of the earth shall be blessed." – Genesis 12:1-4

Abram lost everything because of his love for God. When God Almighty spoke to Abram left it all. He walked away from his family, his inheritance—everything—and he wandered a wilderness chasing after a God he didn't know, but couldn't ignore.

All Abram knew was he was in love with the heart that was behind the voice that promised he would be a blessing to the nations. When God Almighty showed up to Him in Genesis 17, one of the first things He said was that He was going to give him a name. That God did when he changed Abram (exalted father) to Abraham (father of a multitude). Mind you, he did this decades before Abraham had even one child!

> "I make this covenant with you: I promise that you will be the ancestor of many nations. Your name will no longer be Abram, but Abraham, because I am making you the ancestor of many nations."
> – Genesis 17: 4-6

Still to this day, when we say the name Abraham, we automatically put the title "father" in front of it. Admit it, you do! That name "Father of a multitude" defined him. It's the same with you and me. When God gives you a name, it defines you. It becomes your identity and it leads to toward destination or, as Jeremiah 29:11 says in the King James, "an expected end."

Can you pay a great big price for something that is not even mapped out yet? For something you haven't seen, and maybe can't even explain or define? Can you sell out for something simply because you do not have the option to remain where you are? If you are going to follow Jesus, that's exactly what you will have to do. Abraham did.

The Bible tells us Abraham was 75 years old when he left the only home he'd ever known for a land and a destiny he really couldn't even wrap his mind around. He just knew he couldn't stay where he was. He trusted that God was good and had something better for him in that unknown.

Because Abraham was obedient and went after God's promise of a future for him and his descendants, who weren't even born yet and, let's face it, were a long shot as his wife, Sarah, couldn't have children, he was blessed.

> Then the Lord appeared to Abram and said, "To your descendants I will give this land." And there he built an altar to the Lord, who had appeared to him. – Genesis 12:7

All of heaven is ready to applaud your rare courage and your amazing vision for bigger and better when you go after your upgrade just like Abraham did. You have one, you know. God didn't forget to give you a great big destiny. You just have to look for it, like an Easter egg that your loving Daddy hides in plain sight for you to find.

Let Him delight in your search for your life's purpose when you let heaven invade earth through service. Your destiny is the place where His will can be done in and through you.

> And we know that all things work together for good to those who love God; to those who are the called according to His purpose. For whom He foreknew, He also predestined to be conformed to the image of His Son, that He might be the firstborn among many brethren. Moreover whom He predestined, these He also called; whom He called, these He also justified; and whom He justified, these He also glorified.
> – Romans 8:28-30

Through the example of Abraham and his faith journey in the pages you are about to dive into, know that your upgrade is out there. Today is a good day to be like Abraham. Sell out to the unknown of Jesus. Your Kingdom purpose is calling and it's time to go after it. Prophetically put on Abraham's sandals and faithfully follow your feet to that place where all nations will be blessed by your presence on this planet.

– Troy Brewer

Senior Pastor, OpenDoor Church, Burleson, Texas

Bestselling Author of "Redeeming Your Timeline," "Numbers that Preach" and "Looking Up"

Crystal G.H. Lowery

INTRODUCTION

I have been captivated by the study of faith since I was a teenager. Even then, my favorite chapter in the Bible was Hebrews 11. I used to read that chapter over and over, thinking about the greats who are commemorated for their valiant exploits of faith. It is with little coincidence that Abraham is one of my favorite people of all time in the Bible.

We sometimes get caught up in the heroism of Abraham's faith and fact can blur into legend, creating a bigger than life hero. The truly remarkable thing about Abraham is that he was a man, flesh and bones just like us, who used his faith to accomplish great things. He came from one of the worst places and by faith, walked toward the promised land of his destiny. He walked just as you and I walk. But, at a certain point in his life, he exchanged shoes of mediocrity and doubt for sandals of faith. God told Abram to "Leave it all behind" and Abram set off on the road to his destiny with the promise of God and faith that promised to take him step by step.

Abraham's faith journey is beautiful and rugged, full of promise and faith, but full of obstacles that he must overcome. This is life as we know it. Jeremiah 29:11 tells us that God knows the plans He has for us, plans for a hope and a future. Just as God has plans and a destiny for us all, He sure did for Abraham. God led Abraham from the vulgar stench of wickedness to the aroma of an impossible promise.

God is no respecter of persons (Acts 10:34). What he did for Abraham, he will do for each of us. Abraham believed every word of God, trusted Him, learned lessons in the process, but ultimately pulled in the promise into his reality. Enjoy the deep dive as this book will take you on a journey in Abraham's Sandals of Faith!

Crystal G.H. Lowery

PART 1

CHAPTER 1

Abraham the Prophet

Abraham has a plethora of titles. He is a man that is simple, yet deeply complex. Abraham at first thought is known as Father Abraham, the Father of our Faith, the Patriarch. We commonly refer to Abraham's God as the God of Abraham, Isaac, and Jacob and in this way, he is the first in the successive generations of his descendants. However, we don't generally think of Abraham as a prophet. But Abraham was most certainly a prophet.

In fact, Abraham is the first person mentioned in the Bible as a prophet. Although others who lived before him may have acted as a prophet or engaged in prophetic acts, they were never specifically referred to as a prophet.

Understanding Abraham's role and characteristics as a prophet will help us grow in our ability to learn from him and take away truths and keys that will cause us to succeed.

At a certain point in Abraham's faith journey, Abraham and Sarah journeyed to Gerar. There, Abraham instructed Sarah to tell King Abimelech and the people that she was his sister and not his wife. Sarah, even though she was very old herself, was very beautiful and youthful. She was about 89 years old. King Abimelech took Sarah into his harem. It would have been very possible for King Abimelech to take Sarah as his wife.

King Abimelech had a dream where God instructed him to give Sarah back to Abraham because she was his wife. Even though Abimelech's heart was pure in this matter and he had not known she was Abraham's wife, he still was in possession of Sarah. For this even unknown error, even though Abimelech's hands were clean, and his conscience was clear, he and his household and people would suffer. A curse was upon the people causing them to be infertile and barren. God indicated very sternly in the dream that if Abimelech did not return Sarah to Abraham, he would surely die.

The mercy of God was at work for the benefit of Abraham. God told Abimelech that He had not allowed Abimelech to touch Sarah and had kept him from sinning.

What happens next is critical to understand. God now tells Abimelech, "Now return the man's wife, and because he is a prophet, he will intercede on your behalf that you may live. But if you don't give her back – you will certainly die, you and your entire household" (Genesis 20:7 TPT).

Methods of Receiving Revelation as a Prophet

This is the first time that the word prophet is written in the Bible. The Hebrew word here is *navi'*. The meaning of this word means "to bubble up." For many prophets, this is how they receive revelation from the Holy Spirit. It bubbles up in their spirit through the leading of the Holy Spirit. The Hebrew word *navi'* is the most common word for prophet. This can also reference "one who received a divine call." It can also be translated "to declare or one who declares." In some other Semitic languages, the root of this word for prophet means "to call or to proclaim". A similar word in Arabic means "pipe or conduit."[1]

One of the ways that prophets receive revelation from the Lord is that it will bubble up in their spirit and then they can communicate the message to its intended audience. In this way, the prophet is acting as a conduit. They aren't the words of the prophet, but the prophet is speaking the Word of the Lord and is being used as a mouthpiece.

While a prophet is primarily receiving revelation through this bubbling up kind of hearing and then proceeds to speak, there is a sub-species of prophet called a seer. A seer is a seer, that a visual kind of receiver. There are other Hebrew words that describe a seer. I will not go into the depth of that discussion here. My focus here is to look at the meaning of the Hebrew word *navi'* since it is the word used to refer to Abraham as a prophet. I want to examine how Abraham received revelation and how he communicated that revelation. It is important to note that not all prophets are seers, but all seers are prophets. In this vein, I believe that Abraham is a seer prophet.

As I have studied the life of Abraham, in my way of organizing information, I have grouped the encounters that Abraham had with God into ten major encounters. Some of them last longer and have subparts. There are also encounters with other people that affect Abraham, but I have not included those as part of the ten major encounters.

Note for the following Ten Encounters: To make it clearer as to break down information, I have coded God's words to Abraham. <u>Underlined words</u> denote an instruction to Abraham and **bold words** denotes a promise. Also, for these Encounters, the scripture is taken from the Passion Translation (TPT), except where otherwise indicated.

Encounter #1

> Genesis 12:1-3: Original Blessing Prophetic Word with instruction:
>
> <u>Leave it all behind – your native land, your people, your father's household, and go to the land that I will show you. *Follow me*</u>, and I will make you into a great nation. I will exceedingly bless and prosper you, and I will make you famous, so that you will be a

> tremendous source of blessing for others. I will bless all who bless you and curse all who curse you. And through you all the families of the earth will be blessed.
>
> Method of encounter/revelation: God spoke to Abram; God will show Abram (visual) the promised land
>
> Abram's response: obeyed and left
>
> Location: After Terah, Abraham's father, died; in Hara
>
> Note here that Abraham was 75 years old.

This is the first encounter where God speaks to Abram. Abram was in Haran where he had journeyed with his father, Terah, and other family members. Terah had left the city of Ur to go to the land of Canaan. After Terah died, God spoke to Abram. This is the first recorded encounter between God and Abram.

God told Abram to "Leave it all behind." God does know the end from the beginning and he sure did in Abraham's life and legacy. The primary promise God gave to Abram is boldly declared here, "I will make you into a great nation." All the other promises such as promises to exceedingly bless and prosper Abram and to make him famous, to bless those who bless Abram and curse those who curse Abram, as well as all the families of the earth to be blessed are really describing the magnitude of this primary blessing.

Abram is seventy-five years old. Abram does not have biological children. Abram is only one person. He certainly cannot be a great nation in and of himself. However, this epoch promise comes with an initial instruction. "Leave it all behind." Abram must leave his native land, his people, his father's household and go to the land that God would show Abram. Abram must leave the old to receive the new. By leaving the old, Abram also leaves his old self-image, his old ways of doing things, and heads out for the land of promise. Abram will find himself, the true Abram, and through his journey, the mysterious ways of God will be revealed to Abram. The promise is there waiting for Abram, already created for him. For, "As it is written, I have made thee a father of many nations, before him whom he believed, even God, who quickeneth the dead, and calleth those things which be not as though they were" (Romans 4:17 KJV).

God, who is prophetic in His nature and in character knows that one of the keys to receiving the prophetic word is in the word itself. Here God speaks the word to Abram. He calls Abram something he isn't yet in the natural. He speaks forth a promise that looks impossible in a plethora of ways.

Abram is seventy-five years old. Sarai, his wife is about 65. She is well past the age where she can conceive and bear children. They have no children. Their bodies, in terms of reproductive capability, are as good as dead. It appears they are barren and have shown this to be the case.

But God called those things that were not as though they were. God said he would make Abram into a great nation! God tells Abram that he will visually show him the land that his descendants will inherit.

What did Abram do? How did he respond? He obeyed and left. He departed. He not only heard the promise of the Lord, he obeyed the instruction.

Abram is full of new revelation and promise. He knows he will see this promise and that God will keep his eyes sharp to discern and see the promise come to pass.

Encounter #2

> Genesis 12:7: Promise:
>
> **This is the land I will personally deliver to your seed.**
>
> Method of encounter/revelation: God appeared and spoke: God visually showed Abram the land
>
> Abram's response: erected an altar; continued his journey (to Bethel on the east and Ai on the west); built another altar; prayed; worshiped; continued journey to Negev; came back to the altar he built with Bethel on the east and Ai on the west after his experience in Egypt (Gen 13:3-4) (represents returning to his first love).
>
> Location: Shechem, the location of the great oak tree of Moreh

God appeared to Abram and spoke to him. In this encounter, God visually shows Abram the land of promise. Abram sees the land with his own eyes. The promise spoken here is related to the land that will be inherited by Abram's descendants.

It is important to look at the promise and then Abram's response. Abram erected an altar, which we will see him do many times throughout his encounters with God. He built the altar and prayed and worshiped the Lord. The altar is a place of memorial to show reverence and commemorate the time and the encounter with the Lord. It also serves as a memorial when things look impossible to remind us of the sweet presence and powerful promises of the Lord. Altars remind us this about the word of God: "So also will be the word that I speak; it does not return to me unfulfilled. My word performs my purpose and fulfills the mission I sent it out to accomplish." (Isaiah 55:11 TPT)

Shechem

The location of this encounter is in Shechem at the site of the great oak tree of Moreh. The location of encounters with God are important and tells us a lot about the prophetic word and status of the journey. The location of where God speaks or gives revelation is significant. It is not by chance that Abram's second encounter happened here at this grove of oak trees.

At this point, Abram received the orders to leave it all behind and received a major promise of descendants that would inherit the land God would show him. Abram immediately obeyed and left Haran. Here he is in Shechem by the oak of Moreh and receives a promise that confirms and repeats the previous promise. God tells Abram and shows him that this land, what he sees, is what God will personally deliver to his seed.

Abram's second encounter is in a place called Shechem. The meaning of the name Shechem is "shoulder or personal interest". It comes from the Hebrew noun, *shekem*, which means shoulder or the seat of a person's interests.[2]

"This is the land I will personally deliver to your seed." (Genesis 12:7) This is the promise received at Shechem. From the meaning of Shechem, God is also communicating that He has Abram's personal interest in mind. He is shouldering the burden of the promise He made to Abram. God is carrying the words he spoke to Abram and protecting their harvest. Those words will be redeemed, and Abram will not be ignored or passed over anymore. One negative connotation for shoulder is used in the phrase "cold shoulder" which refers to being ignored or having someone turn their face from you. God is turning his face toward Abram with this promise and no longer will Abram be without seed. God will bear or shoulder the promise of Abram's seed to mature into a bountiful harvest.

It is also very much in alignment with the promise here that Shechem means "Personal Interest". God has taken a personal interest in Abram's life, in his legacy, and in the promise, He has spoken to Abram. The very promise is that God will PERSONALLY deliver this land to Abram's seed. God is making this personal. God is not far away and impersonal. He is very close, very present, and very in touch with our lives.

Abram is learning and growing in his journey with God, in his faith walk, in his relationship with God. Abram is learning that God speaks to him one on one. God speaks promises, but also gives instructions. God directs and instructs to lead him to where he needs to be. God is very personally involved in the promises He speaks and shoulders them to fulfillment.

Abram's descendant, Jesus, will one day bear the responsibility of complete dominion which will rest on his shoulders.

A child has been born for us; a son has been given to us.

The responsibility of *complete* dominion

will rest on his shoulders, and his name will be: The Wonderful One!

The Extraordinary Strategist! The Mighty God!

The Father of Eternity! The Prince of Peace!

Great and vast is his dominion.

He will bring immeasurable peace and prosperity.

He will rule on David's throne and over David's kingdom

to establish and uphold it by promoting justice and righteousness from this time forward and forevermore.

The marvelous passion that the Lord Yahweh, Commander of Angel Armies, has for his people will ensure that it is finished!

Isaiah 9:6-8 TPT

Oak of Moreh

The oak of Moreh was near Shechem. This is where Abram built an altar to God after he arrived in Canaan and had the second encounter. After his time at the oak of Moreh, Abram will go to Bethel for a stay. Bethel means "House of God". As we have seen, Abram is not simply wandering around. He is on a specific course that God has mapped out for his journey. He is at the beginning of his journey here and marks the commemoration with an altar.

I live in the south. Here, oak trees are iconic. They are well known with their picturesque Spanish Moss which drapes from their branches. Oak trees are used in logos especially in southern culture because they relate to the southern landscape and because they manifest the feeling of strength and durability.

Oak means, "longevity; stable (deeply rooted); Kingdom pillar (landmark); the Cross; place to shelter; place to bury the past; durable (used for oars); and strong".[3] It is no coincidence that this particular tree is where Abram received additional revelation from God. All the meanings of the word oak are relevant here. The promise God has given to Abram to give his seed, his descendants, the promised land is not a flimsy statement. It is not without backing or substance. This promise bears the making of a dynasty for Abram. As we will see later, God will promise not just a nation to Abram, but he will be the father of nations. There will be so many descendants, just as numerous as the stars in the sky and the sand on the seashore. God will use the birth and maturing of this promise to Abram to fulfill His purposes in the earth, to build His Kingdom, eventually bringing about the birth of the Messiah to be the King of this Kingdom. The oak tree here signifies to Abram that within this promise, he is a Kingdom pillar, and that Abram will be a landmark that his future descendants will point to as their beginning point, but not their ending point. God is surely saying to Abram that life will not end in the body of Abram himself, but that there is living seed within Abram that will multiply and flourish.

We see that the Cross is a meaning of the oak. From Abram's most prominent descendant, Jesus, the Cross would be carried and would one day be the symbol, the crossroads where life reigns over death. Just as we saw in one of the meanings of the name Shechem, "shoulder", here the oak confirms that just as God would shoulder the weight and burden of carrying the promise he made to Abram, here he will shelter Abram. We see God's provision of sheltering Abram throughout his journey in keeping and preserving him. Here Abram buries the past by moving forward, in obeying the instruction he receives from God. The initial encounter with God came with the instruction to "Leave it all behind." Abram has obeyed faithfully. For Abram to move forward and to find himself and what he will truly be, he must bury the dead, his past, in order to receive his future, the promise of life. The only way to move forward in the journey of faith is to stand strong in the word of the Lord and commit wholeheartedly, trusting that what He says is true. Oak trees have been used to make oars because of their durability. The strength and durability of the oar allows for the boat to keep moving forward in the face of a current of opposition. It will behoove Abram to hold on to the oars of faith because they will prove to take Abram to the land of promise. God's word and promises are unbreakable. In the Psalms, David says, "Forever, O Lord, thy word is settled in heaven [stands firm as the heavens]" (Psalms 119:89 AMP).

Abram is still early in his faith journey. God is teaching him to trust fully, to not hold back, and to obey immediately. The oak was at Moreh and is referred to as the oak of Moreh. The meaning of Moreh is "Teacher".[4]

God is strengthening his relationship during this time in his role as

Teacher to his student, Abram. There are lessons Abram needs to learn, instruction he needs to receive, and tests he needs to pass. He has just started his course in faith. As with any student, he will be successful because His Teacher is fully vested in the outcome of His pupil.

Another meaning of Moreh is "Early Rain". [5] Early rain is rain that falls during the first part of the agricultural year. This is the time when seeds are planted, but they have not sprouted yet. They have been sown, but the eye cannot see any growth. In this second encounter with God, the promise given is "This is the land I will personally deliver to your seed." It is interesting that the word "seed" is used here to refer to the promise of descendants. Moreh is a reminder that God has spoken his promise and it will not return empty. The seed has been sown and the early rain has fallen on the newly planted seedling. The seedling is receiving the water and is nourishing it in just the perfect soil.

"Early Rain" can also refer to the daily work of the Spirit of God instructing, teaching, and leading. Such early rain tends to the seed providing security and nourishment so that it will germinate.[6] This early rain will cause revival or resurrection in what was already dead in Abram's life since he and Sarai were both well past age to conceive and bear children. It will show the favor of God and cause fruitfulness because of the power in the Word of God itself.

There is a time period between the sowing of the seed and the harvesting of the crop. Here, Abram must look at the land (the visual God has given him), the soil, ahead of him and recognize that in this earth, the plantings are being soaked with life and they will grow and mature into the very thing that was planted. This is a powerful reminder that a harvest will surely come because "as long as the earth exists there will always be seasons of planting and harvest" (Genesis 8:22 TPT).

Encounter #3

> Genesis 13:14-18: Promise with Instruction
>
> <u>Lift up your eyes and look around you to the north, the south, the east, and the west.</u> As far as you can see in every direction is the land that I will give to you forever – to you and your seed. I will multiply them until they are as numerous as the specks of dust on the earth. If anyone could count the dust of the earth, then your offspring could also be counted. <u>Now, get up and walk through the land – its length and its breadth.</u> *All the land you walk upon* will be my gift to you!
>
> Method of encounter/revelation: God spoke
>
> Abram's response: moved his camp and settled by the oaks of Mamre, which are at Hebron; built altar
>
> Location: When Abram settled in the land of Canaan (and after Lot separated from him).

One of the most significant aspects of this encounter is that it happens after Lot separated from Abram. After this separation, God speaks to Abram again. It is apparent that God had to wait to provide further blessing and instruction to Abram until he was free of Lot by his side. There is much more to be said about this aspect of separation that brings about revelation, but this will be saved for a later chapter.

Here, God speaks to Abram again. So far, God's method of providing revelation and blessing to Abram is through his voice to Abram. In some ways, this is a continuation of the previous blessing. Again, God instructs Abram to look at what is before his eyes. His instructions are to look in all directions – to the north, south, east, and west. In every possible direction and for as far as Abram can see is the land that God promises to give to Abram forever. To make it very clear as far as the magnitude of this blessing, God tells Abram to look up and lift his eyes. Through this visual, God is making sure that Abram takes in the scope and scale of the blessing and let it settle and become real and tangible in his mind. God tells Abram that his descendants will be so numerous that they won't be able to be counted just as it is impossible to count the specks of dust on the earth.

After seeing this vast land before his eyes, God instructs Abram to get up and walk through the land – its length and breadth. This is the first time since God instructed Abram to leave it all behind that Abram must physically do something. Instead of staying put or sitting down, it is necessary to get up from that place. Abram must rise to the occasion and get ready for the blessing to manifest. God tells Abram to walk through the land. He must walk through the blessing, take a tour, and get familiar with what he is promised. By setting his feet on the land he is physically taking dominion and control and authority over the promise. It is under his feet. Wherever Abram walked, wherever his feet touched is coming into the package of the promise. Symbolically and prophetically, the blessing will be enlarged the more he walks through the land.

Abram does obey God in these instructions. Afterward, Abram moved his camp, his dwelling place and settled by the oaks of Mamre, which are in Hebron. There, he built another altar to the Lord. In encounter #2, we discussed the prophetic meaning of oak. Here, we have more oaks and they are at a place called Mamre, which means "well -fed or fatness".[7]

Here we see painted a picture of the strength of God's oil being poured on Abram, the anointing. These are not lean promises, but they are full of the fatness of God's blessing and the weighty glory of the Lord drenching Abram with promises of blessing.

Encounter #4

> Genesis 14:18 –20: Special Blessing
>
> **Blessed is Abram by God Most High, Creator of heaven and earth. And blessed be God Most High, whose power delivered your enemies into your hands!**
>
> Method of encounter/revelation: Melchizedek walked out and spoke and brought bread and wine (communion).
>
> Abram's response: gave 10% of all his assets (not just income); also told King of Sodom he would not take the spoils of war for himself because he had raised his hand to Yahweh and pledged a solemn oath that he would keep nothing for himself so it would be clear that only the Lord had caused him to increase in wealth.
>
> Location: Valley of the Shaveh (known as the King's Valley and later became known as the Kidron Valley).

This encounter is a different type of encounter than the previous ones. Whereas before God spoke to Abram with promises and sometimes instructions, here we see something different. We see a mystery man named Melchizedek come onto the scene to greet Abram with bread and wine, just after Abram has returned from defeating some kings who had captured Lot and all Lot's possessions.

Encounter number three happens just after Lot separates from Abram. Encounter number four happens just after Abram redeems

Lot and his possessions. Abram recovers all the stolen possessions and brings back Lot as well as all the women and prisoners. Even though Abram has rescued Lot and brought him safely back, they do stay separate. Abram does not invite Lot to come and dwell with him again as he had before the separation of the two. It does show the integrity and character of Abram that even with Lot's cleaving to old ways, old ideas, old gods and continuing to live in Sodom, Abram still was concerned for his welfare and safety. Abram saw that justice was served and rescued Lot to safety along with his worldly possessions.

Of importance in this encounter is the location which takes place at the valley of the Shaveh which was known as the King's Valley and later known as the Kidron Valley. The word "Shaveh" means "level or equal as in equalize". We see that what has just happened is that Abram has leveled the field in defeating his enemies which were initially Lot's enemies. This valley had several names which are significant. Also known as the King's Valley, the meaning, which is very significant in Abram's encounter, signifies the low place, where we meet the King.[8] Abram has learned on his faith journey that to meet God, his King, he must bow himself. So many times, after Abram has encounters with God, he immediately builds an altar to pray and worship the Lord. At these altars, he kneels and in this low place meets the King!

It is in this place of humility that Abram is greeted by Melchizedek. We see that Melchizedek has bread and wine for Abram, the communion. This is pointing to Jesus, who we remember, when we take communion. The bread representing Jesus' body which was broken for us and the wine representing the blood of Jesus which paid for all our sin. This is obviously pointing and looking forward to Jesus, as Jesus has not been born yet. What is the significance of Melchizedek bringing the communion to Abram just after he returns from rescuing Lot? We will examine this in further detail next.

The Bible never expresses that Lot was unrighteous. However, Lot did not cleave to his uncle Abram. When Lot was faced with a decision to take one part of the land to support and sustain his people and livestock, he did not choose Abram. It would have been in Lot's best interest to make the choice to stay with Abram because God was with Abram. It was clear that Abram was living in the favor and blessing of the Lord. However, Lot did not stay under the covering of Abram, where there was protection and anointing. He was not living in the will of God by separating himself from Abram. The meaning of the name "Lot" is "covert, secret, or concealed". [9] Lot had never really left Ur in the past even though he was physically in a different location. He took the ways and mindsets and was still living in that place of the past.

Knowing his nephew's choice, how he had fallen short, and was still living in what God wanted Abram to leave behind, Abram had compassion and mercy on Lot. Still seeing his compromising ways, Abram chose to take 318 men to go and take back his family member. Abram could easily have made the choice to let Lot suffer his consequences.

Jesus was completely perfect, never falling short, never compromising or disobeying His Father. From the beginning, this perfect God-man, was purposed to be the substitution for us, to be the one whose body was broken and beaten and whose blood was shed for our unrighteousness. The taking of communion here by Abram and administered by Melchizedek is fitting because it is a picture of what Abram did for Lot, but even more so, pointing us to the masterpiece of the finished work of Jesus.

Some believe Melchizedek was just a man. This passage does give us some information about him. He was both a priest of God Most High and also the king of Salem. "Salem" means "peace". So, he was a king of peace. I have included this meeting as an encounter because I believe that Melchizedek was more than a man, but a pre-incarnate appearance of Christ. There are many reasons I believe this and that would be a much longer discussion than allowed for here in this chapter. Let me just provide a brief few points as to why I believe this is the case.

Jesus was both a king and a priest, just as Melchizedek was. Jesus was also a prophet, holding a third office.

Melchizedek's name means king of righteousness which perfectly describes Jesus. Melchizedek was, as a person, unrighteous. However, Jesus was the only righteous person to ever live and is the only perfect and righteous King.

Melchizedek was king of Salem. As we discussed earlier, this means "king of peace". As every story and every word of the Bible points us to Jesus, this surely is pointing us to Jesus, who is our Prince of Peace. Jesus reconciled us to God and closed the gap between us because of sin and unrighteousness.

This passage says that Melchizedek was a priest of God Most High or El Elyon. Even though the Bible does not tell us about his functions, we know that Jesus, as God's divine Son, was the ultimate and perfect priest of God Most High.

Jesus is an eternal priest who lives forever. We learn in Hebrews some interesting facts about Melchizedek. He "has no father or mother, and no record of any of his ancestors. He was never born, and he never died, but his life is like a picture of the Son of God, a King-Priest forever" (Hebrews 7:3 TPT)!

Melchizedek just appears and then disappears. For all the reasons above, I do believe he is a divine being, most likely pre-incarnate Christ. Therefore, this is definitely an encounter that Abram is having here in the King's Valley.

Melchizedek delivered a very special blessing over Abram. He says that God Most High has blessed Abram and has allowed Abram to defeat his enemies![10]

The very next thing that happens is that Abram gives Melchizedek a tenth of all he possessed. There is enumerated detail in Hebrews 7:4-10 about the tithe. Tithe means "tenth". Today, we think of a tithe as a tenth of our income. However, it is an important note here that Abram gave not just from his income, but of all he possessed – all his portfolio!

Just after the tithe is given, the King of Sodom suggested to Abram to keep the spoils of the war for himself. However, Abram tells him that he cannot do this because he has vowed to Yahweh and pledged a solemn oath that he will not keep anything for himself that belongs to you (King of Sodom), not even a thread of a garment. This way, the King of Sodom will never be able to say that he made Abram rich. It will be clear that ONLY God blessed Abram and made him rich.

This is interesting because this is what the tithe represents. When we tithe and give God the first ten percent of our income (even though Abram gave of his entire assets), we are giving to God what is God's. If we keep that and withhold the tithe, then we are stealing what is not ours. Just as Abram tells the King of Sodom, he cannot keep what belongs to the King of Sodom, we cannot keep what belongs to God. God will bless the ninety percent and cause us to increase in wealth.

Abram did not withhold from Melchizedek (Christ) or man (King of Sodom) what was theirs and not his. He gave the tithe, and he gave the spoils. He could easily have kept but he gave. His hand was open to give and God will make sure that while his hand is open, he will continue to receive.

Encounter #5

Encounter 5.1:

Genesis 15:1-21 – entire chapter (Multipart encounter)

Genesis 15:1-3: promise with instruction

<u>Abram, don't yield to fear</u>, **for I am your Faithful Shield and your Abundant Reward.**

Method of encounter/revelation: Vision and God Spoke

Abram's response: replied with a question

Location: Abram's tent

Encounter 5.2:

Genesis 15:4: promise

No! Eliezer will not be your heir. I will give you a son from your own body to be your heir.

Method of encounter/revelation: Abram's response:

Location: Abram's tent

Encounter 5.3:

Genesis 15:5: promise with instruction

<u>Gaze into the night sky. Go ahead and try to count the stars.</u> **Your seed will be as numerous as the stars!**

Method of encounter/revelation: God brought Abram outside his tent and spoke

Abram's response: trusted every word God had spoken (And because of his faith, God credited it to him as righteousness.)

Location: Abram's tent, but then God brought Abram outside his tent

Encounter 5.4:

Genesis 15:7: promise

I am Yahweh, who brought you out of the Babylonian city of Ur, to give you and all this land to possess.

Method of encounter/revelation: God spoke

Abram's response: asked a question

Location: outside Abram's tent.

Encounter 5.5:

Genesis 15:9: instruction

<u>Bring me a heifer, a female goat, and a ram, each three years old, also a turtledove and a young pigeon.</u>

Method of encounter/revelation: God spoke

Abram's response: brought animals, killed them, cut them in two, laid each half opposite the other in two rows (Vultures swooped down upon the carcasses, but Abram stood there and drove the vultures away)

Location: outside Abram's tent

Encounter 5.6:

Genesis 15:12-16: promise

Know this: Your descendants will live as strangers in a foreign country. They will be enslaved and mistreated for four hundred years. Afterward I will punish that nation for enslaving them, and your descendants will come out of slavery with untold wealth. You, however, will go to your ancestors in peace and live a full life. And after the fourth generation, your descendants will return here; for then the sin of the Amorites will be ripe for judgment.

Method of encounter/revelation: God spoke while Abram was in a deep state of sleep

Abram's response: He listened

Location: Most likely outside Abram's tent since the text does not say he went back into his tent. Also, starting in verse 17, it says that it was very dark when there appeared a smoking firepot and a blazing torch that passed between the carcasses (his sacrifices).

Encounter 5.7:

Genesis 15:17-21: promise

I have given this land to your descendants, from the Egyptian border to the great river Euphrates, the entire land of the Kenites, the Kenizzites, the Kadmonites, the Hittites, the Perizzites, the Rephaites, the Amorites, the Canaanites, the Girgashites, and the Jebusites.

Method of encounter/revelation: Suddenly appeared a smoking firepot and a blazing torch that passed between the split carcasses; God entered into covenant with Abram and spoke

Abram's response: He listened and watched

Location: Most likely outside Abram's tent because the text says it was very dark when there appeared a smoking firepot and a blazing torch that passed between the carcasses (his sacrifices).

This encounter happens in seven different parts, which I have broken down for ease of study. Abram has just defeated the enemy kings and rescued Lot and his possessions and has been met by

Melchizedek, taken communion, and paid a tithe to Melchizedek. After all this, Abram has the next encounter.

Abram has his first vision, and the word of God came to him. God instructs him not to yield to fear and promises that He is Abram's Faithful Shield and his Abundant Reward. How very timely and relevant this is to Abram, who could potentially let fear seep in regarding any possible threat of revenge from these enemy kings he has just conquered. Abram was very noble and courageous to take his men and fight for his nephew Lot. Abram has been protected, not of his own strength, but because he has been behind The Shield of Who is faithful. God promises to remain Abram's Faithful Shield. I believe that God was telling Abram that not only was He protecting Abram in the previous battle, but He will continue to protect Abram in any future battles, even ones he doesn't yet know about.

God also promises Abram that He is Abram's Abundant Reward. Abram has just been faithful and honoring with his assets. He has given Melchizedek a tenth of his assets. Abram has also not kept any of the spoils of war as a trophy reward. He has been full of integrity concerning material things. God is rewarding Abram and promising Him that even though Abram has given up worldly wealth, God is worth far more than what he has given. God IS his reward, not the material wealth. Not only will Abram have an intimate relationship with Yahweh, but Yahweh will reward him with overflowing wealth, spiritually, materially, and also in his family line.

Abram responded to God with a question asking what good is this reward if he does not have a son? Abram is concerned that he has yet to see himself with the tangible evidence of a son and that his servant will be his beneficiary instead.

God spoke again to Abram. He confirms that Eliezer, Abram's

servant, will not be Abram's heir, but that it will surely be the promised son of Abram. Up until this point, Abram has been receiving this revelation while he was inside his tent. Here, God takes Abram outside of his tent and then continues speaking to Abram. The transition from inside to outside his tent is pivotal in terms of the step-up in revelation Abram will receive from God.

Abram's tent represents his human body, his physical limitations, his mental limitations, and his faith limitations. In a later chapter, we will explore this in further detail. Abram has just questioned God about having a biological son even though God has promised this to him. Abram did not doubt God, but he did question God about this promise.

God instructs Abram to gaze into the night sky and try and count the stars. Abram's natural vision is filled with the wonder and expanse in picture form of what God is promising him. Abram could not have seen this vast and majestic display of stars from inside his tent. He had to leave his tent, this confining space that is comfortable, but with definite dimensions that are set. He had to leave the tent with a visual impairment to be able to clearly look up and see this promise. Here he is able to look up instead of at looking at himself to see the reality of what the Creator of the universe can speak forth.

Something so beautiful happens next. The passage says that, "And Abram trusted every word Yahweh had spoken" (Genesis 15:6 TPT)! How could Abram do this? He had grown in intimacy with God. He had received the promise of Yahweh as being his Abundant Reward. Through his ever- deepening relationship with God, his vision had been expanded and he was able to reflect on what God had already created. If God can create the stars in the night sky, it would be nothing for him to provide Abram with a son. Stepping outside of his tent, Abram left the boundaries of his faith and walked into the limitless boundaries of faith in God. Abram trusted every word that God had spoken.

"In the beginning [before all time] was the Word (Christ), and the Word was with God, and the Word was God Himself. He was [continually existing] in the beginning [co-eternally] with God. All things were made *and* came into existence through Him; and without Him not even one thing was made that has come into being. In Him was life [and the power to bestow life], and the life was the Light of men. The Light shines on in the darkness, and the darkness did not understand it *or* overpower it *or* appropriate it *or* absorb it [and is unreceptive to it] (I John 1:1-5 AMP)".

This passage explains what we have just seen in Abram's faith journey. He has grown deep in his relationship with God and has trusted His every word. We understand that in I John above, Jesus IS the Word. So, Abram was actually trusting in Jesus, in every word spoken by God. He was visually looking at the expanse of the universe, created by the Word, who was and is continually existing with God. It is interesting that God showed Abram the night sky with the stars shining brightly. This passage goes on to say that The Light shines on in the darkness. But in Him (Jesus) was Life and that Life is the Light of men. Seeing the brightly shining stars signifies just how much life was going to result from God's promise – Abram's descendants would be as numerous as the stars in the sky.

"And because of his faith, Yahweh credited it to him as righteousness." (Genesis 15:6 TPT) There is an exchange that takes place here. Think of Abram as having a heavenly account, like an earthly financial account where you make deposits and withdrawals. God deposited or credited righteousness into Abram's account because of Abram's faith. Abram didn't just have little faith. "Abram trusted every word Yahweh had spoken," (Genesis 15:6 TPT) and this is the faith God saw. Abram obviously had absolutely nothing in the natural to believe in for this promise. In fact, every circumstance in the natural was against the promise. Abram was elderly; Sarai was also very old and at least a few decades past being able to conceive children. However, despite what his physical eyes could see, and his mind could reason, Abram chose to believe and trust every word of the promise of God to him.

Because of his faith, Abram was credited righteousness to his account. This means that when God looked at Abram, he was right and perfect before God. Abram did not work for this righteousness to be credited to him. He only believed. He only trusted. He only put his faith in every word of God.

Righteousness was a gift to Abram and with this gift, he was made right before God. Righteousness is still a gift today for you and me. When we have faith in Jesus and receive him into our lives, we can receive that gift of righteousness as well. "For when we believe and embrace the One who brought our Lord Jesus back to life, perfect righteousness will be credited to our account as well (Romans 4:24 TPT)."

Righteousness is having right standing before God. When you have righteousness, you can stand before the higher authority to present your case. In my legal practice, I encounter the issue of standing frequently. The legal definition of "Standing" is that a person or party has the capacity, has met the requirements, to bring their case before a particular court. For example, in a probate situation where a person has died and we need to administer that decedent's estate, we will open a probate estate in a particular county. There are factors we need to consider before filing the case. For example, where did the decedent live (county of residence), where did the decedent die, and where are the assets located (specifically all real estate)? These are some of the questions we answer to find out where we will have standing before the proper court.

There was one requirement for Abram. It was faith. It was because of Abram's faith that righteousness was credited to him and it is still by faith for us today!

Abram, in his conversation with God, asked God for confirmation of how he could be sure that he would really possess the land of promise? Abram is really asking God here for some legal authority to know that he can stake his claim and know he has the title deed to this land. Abram, in legal terms, is asking to present his case in the court of equity before God as judge in his suit to quiet title. I am currently representing a plaintiff in a suit to quiet title on a piece of real estate that was purchased in the late 1800s by the great-grandfather of the plaintiff. The great-grandfather passed and verbally indicated the real estate was to be passed to a particular child. That child began paying property taxes, but the title was never updated to reflect the new owner. This owner verbally conveyed the real estate to one of his children. The same thing happened for multiple generations. The last recorded title deed to the property was recorded almost 140 years ago. Now, we are asking for the court to quiet the title and sign a deed which we dill draft conveying the title to the great-granddaughter. Of course, there is a long list of requirements and formalities we must meet before we get to the Judge signing the order and the deed being signed. However, the plaintiff has standing to present her case in this particular court, and we are very confident that she will receive a clear title to the property.

Abram can present his case before God because of his faith in every single word that God spoke to him. Because of Abram's faith, he has been credited with righteousness and now has right standing before God. He can, through this suit to quiet title, get a clean and clear title deed to the promised land which has been ordered by the court and signed by the Judge.

After Abram asked God about this issue of standing, God gave Abram some instructions. He told Abram to bring a heifer, a female goat, a ram, as well as a turtledove and young pigeon and sacrifice them to the Lord. Abram did as he was told. Abram divided the appropriate animals in two and sacrificed them. Abram continues to just obey the instructions of the Lord. Even Jesus had to obey his Father to be proven perfect. "But even though he was a wonderful Son, he learned to listen and obey through all his sufferings. And after being proven perfect in this way he has now become the source of eternal salvation to all those who listen to him and obey (Hebrews 5:8-9 TPT)".

Something we learn here in the death or sacrifice of these animals to God is that suffering precedes inheritance. God instructed Abram in his infinite wisdom to sacrifice these animals. Abram obeyed. God knew this would precede Abram receiving the title deed he had just brought before God as Judge. As we saw in the passage above, Jesus also obeyed his Father and through his sufferings (his sacrifice on the cross), we now have the inheritance of eternal salvation and the fullness of the blessings of God.

As the process of the sacrifice was taking place, it is interesting that vultures swooped down to take the carcasses. However, Abram stood there and drove them away. Abram has been contending for the promise for a while. He is fighting his good fight of faith. He has his faith shield on and is prepared for this battle. Ephesians 6:15 TPT says, "In every battle, take faith as your wrap-around shield, for it is able to extinguish the blazing arrows coming at you from the Evil One!" The vultures, I believe, represent the enemy's attempt to steal from Abram his ability to follow through in his obedience to the instruction of the Lord to disqualify him from his inheritance. However, Abram did something resilient. He stood. He drove them away. This reminds me of a powerful reminder that Paul wrote in Ephesians 6:13 (KJV), "Therefore, take unto you the whole armor of God, that ye may be able to withstand in the evil day and, having done all, to stand." When you have done everything and the battle is still going on, keep standing. Abram has been obeying God, following his commands, listening to every word He speaks, believing every single word, and he is still waiting and believing in faith for the promise. He is continuing to obey and based on his obedience, inheritance will come, but the enemy is doing his job and trying to sabotage Abram's obedience. Despite this resistance and attack of the enemy, Abram has on his armor for battle and especially his shield of faith and he continued to stand and defeat the vultures of evil.

That night, a deep darkness fell, and Abram went into a sleep that was a trance-like state. In this state, God spoke to Abram. God assured Abram that he would have descendants. In fact, God spoke to Abram about some events that would take place for more than four hundred years out into the future. God told him that his descendants would live in a foreign land as slaves and that they would be delivered after four hundred years. God is speaking to Abram about the time the Israelites would live as slaves in Egypt. God prophesied to Abram that when the Israelites leave this land of slavery, they would be compensated with untold wealth for their years of mistreatment. God also assured Abram that he would go and die in peace and live a full life. We know that Abram lived to be 175. Lastly, God assured Abram that his descendants would come back to inherit the land after they left Egypt.

We find out that at this point, the sun had set, and it was very dark outside. A strange part of this encounter occurs here. Suddenly, a smoking firepot and a blazing torch appeared and passed between the split sacrifices. God can encounter us in any way he pleases. We have seen Abram's encounters be the voice of God, visions, dreams, but here, we see something entirely different. God's presence showed up in the form of a smoking firepot and a blazing torch. These two forms point us to two persons of God, the Father, and the Son. Something beautiful will happen as well going forward. The manifest presence of God walking between the split carcasses points to the future when the same God will show himself and walk in the land with Abram and his descendants to fully conquer what is rightfully theirs.

God spoke to Abram here and gives him what he has just brought before the court. Abram receives the title deed to the land. The title is quieted with these words from Yahweh: "I have given this land to your descendants, from the Egyptian border to the great river Euphrates, the entire land of the Kenites, the Kenizzites, the Kadmonites, the Hittites, the Perizzites, the Rephaites the Amorites, the Canaanites, the Girgashites, and the Jebusites" (Genesis 15:18-21 TPT). Here we have the boundaries to the promised land or what we call on a title to real estate, the legal description. The legal description gives the metes and bounds or the exact borders and dimensions of the real estate.

This encounter has been full of wonderful revelations, lessons in obedience, and the gift of righteousness. We see that Abram's petition in court was indeed granted. He had standing to present his case before God as Righteous Judge, was credited righteousness because of his faith, and the Judge signed the court order, and the title has been quieted. Abram has the title in his hand. It has been signed. It has been recorded. It is in the public records for all heaven and earth to see.

Encounter #6

> Encounter 6.1:
>
> 17:1: Promise
>
> I am the God who is more than enough. Live your life in my presence and be blameless. I will confirm my covenant between me and you, and will greatly multiply your descendants.
>
> Method of encounter/revelation: God appeared and spoke Abram's

response: fell his face in awe before God Location: land of Canaan

Note: Abram was 99 years old

Encounter 6.2:

17:3: Promise with instruction

I establish my covenant with you: "You will become a father of many nations. You will no longer be named Abram because I am changing your name to Abraham, For I have made you a father of many nations. I will make you abundantly fruitful, more than you expect. I will make nations out of you, and kings will trace their lineage back to you. Yes, I will establish my eternal covenant of love between me and you, and it will extend to your descendants throughout their generations. I will be your children's God, just as I am your God. I will give to you and your seed the land to which you have migrated. The entire land of Canaan will be yours and your descendants as an everlasting possession. <u>And I will be their God forever!</u>

Your part of the covenant is to obey its terms, you and your descendants throughout the ages. So here is the sign of the covenant that you are to keep, so that it will endure between you and me and your descendants: Circumcise every male among you. You must undergo cutting off the flesh of your foreskin as a special sign of the covenant between me and you. Throughout the generations, each male child must be circumcised eight days after his birth. This includes those not of your descendants —

those born in your household and foreign-born servants whom you have purchased; they must be circumcised, homeborn and purchased alike. In this way, you will carry in the flesh the sign of my everlasting covenant. Any uncircumcised male who does not have the foreskin of his flesh cut off, will be cut off from his people for he has broken my covenant.

Concerning your wife Sarai, you are not to call her Sarai anymore, but Sarah, My Princess, will be her name. I will wonderfully bless her, and I will certainly give you a son through her. Yes, I will bless her greatly, and she will become a mother of nations; kings of nations will arise among her children!

Method of encounter/revelation: God spoke

Location: Land of Canaan

Abraham's response: He laughed so hard he fell to the ground (at the prospect of Sarah having a baby at her age) and then spoke (instead asking God to bless Ishmael.

Encounter 6.3:

17:19-27: Promise with instruction

Listen to me. I promise that you and Sarah will have a son, **and you will call him Isaac.** I will confirm my everlasting covenant of love with him and his seed. And regarding Ishmael, I have heard your cry and I will indeed bless him. I will cause him to have many, many descendants. He will father twelve rulers, and I will make him into

> a great nation. But my everlasting covenant relationship is with Isaac, who will be born to you and Sarah about this time next year.
>
> Method of encounter/revelation: God spoke and when finished ascended into heaven
>
> Abraham's response: without delay obeyed, took Ishmael and every male, and circumcised them that very day; Abraham was 99, Ishmael was 13; they were both circumcised that same day.
>
> Location: land of Canaan

There is a long silence in the encounters Abram has with God. The Bible does not give us the reason for this silence, but only the amount of time of no further revelation. We know that Abram was 75 years old when he had his first encounter with God. We have some further information in Genesis chapter 16 about Abram's age when Ishmael was born. He was 86 years old when Hagar gave birth to Ishmael. That is told to us in the last verse of Genesis chapter 16. In the first verse of chapter 17, we find out that Abram is now 99 years old. There is at least a 13-year lapse of encounter with God. Since we do not know how old Abram was in his last encounter (encounter #5), we don't know the time from that encounter to when Ishmael was born. So, we can just say there was more than 13 years of silence.

This is intriguing for a few reasons. We know Abram was a prophet. We tend to assume that because of his position and role as a prophet, he would receive continual encounters and revelation from God. However, we see this is not the case. We also read similar patterns of encounters that other prophets in the Bible had as well as from living prophets in our current day.

The break in encounter did not mean that Abram was no longer a prophet. It also did not mean that Abram was not going to receive his promise. We do know that the last event that happened which was recorded prior to this encounter was that Abram listened to Sarai and took Hagar with the hopes of having a son. In Genesis 16:6 TPT, we find out what Sarai said and what Abram did in response: "Perhaps through her I can build you a family. Abram listened and did what Sarai asked." Sarai said something interesting here and it is that she thought if she had a Plan B, which was Hagar, that she could help the promise of God come to pass. The words "I can build you..." in this verse point to the true state of Sarai's heart. "For what has been stored up in your hearts will be heard in the overflow of your words" (Matthew 12:34 TPT). She was trying to cause the promise to come about in her own strength, to build Abram a family through her own scheme and strategy. Abram's response is the mark of a good husband who wants to keep the peace with his wife! He listened and did what Sarai asked.

I don't think that it is the fact that Abram did take Hagar to be his second wife and that she conceived Ishmael that is the problem. It was customary in those days to have multiple wives and to take the servant women of the primary wife if that wife was barren. However, the problem here is of the heart. "Guard your heart above all else, for it determines the course of your life." (Proverbs 4:23 NLT) These are wise words to protect your life and destiny. We can see in the words Sarai spoke what was truly in her heart. There were some flesh works evident instead of God works. Abram listened to Sarai's heart and did what she asked. Even though he already had 5 intimate encounters with God, he still listened to the voice of Sarai and acted on her words instead of the words God had spoken to him. By his actions of consent to Sarai's heart, he is aligning his heart with her's and so the act of Abram taking Hagar to be his secondary wife who conceived Ishmael is a work of the flesh and is rebellion and sin against the words of God.

It therefore is an interesting statement by God to be silent for 13 years after this act. The number thirteen means rebellion and sin. It signifies the flesh rising up to control something. Some other references to the number thirteen are that Nimrod was the 13th generation from Adam. Nimrod was a terrorist and is the builder of Babylon, which is the world's modus operandi instead of God's way or the Kingdom mindset. Also, Ishmael, who we have seen as the son of the flesh, was circumcised when he was 13 years old. It is also interesting that Solomon took only 7 years to build the Temple, but took 13 years to build his own house.[11]

I do believe that these 13 years of silence tell us that God saw Abram's act of the flesh and was disappointed in his sin. If Abram had not succumbed to his flesh, imagine the encounters he could have had with the Lord during this 13-year dry period. However, God is merciful and full of grace. After this time of silence, God speaks to Abram again.

Abram is now 99 years old. Since his first encounter at age 75, 24 years have gone by. Sarai is now 89 and Ishmael is 13. Yahweh appeared to Abram and spoke to him. I can only imagine that Abram has noticed his lack of hearing from God for years and has often been sorry for taking the plan in his own hands. How wonderful it must have been for Abram to have had God appear to him and speak to him, lead him from Ur and journey at least 500 miles, defeat kings, and experience supernatural encounters like smoking firepots and blazing torches.

How Abram must have missed this intimacy with the Lord. His heart must have cried out to the Lord for a return of that closeness. Now, for the first time in a marked time of silence, Abram sees and hears God again. The words God spoke are so beautiful. They show His continued faithfulness, love, mercy, and abundance that covers Abram. "I am the God who is more than enough. Live your life in my presence and be blameless. I will confirm my covenant between me and you, and I will greatly multiply your descendants." (Genesis 17:1-2 TPT)

God gives Abram one of his names which is El Shaddai. This name has multiple meanings. It can mean "God of the Holy Mountain," "God of the Wilderness," "God the Destroyer of Enemies," "God the All-Sufficient One," "God the Nurturer of Babies (the Breasted One)," "God the Almighty," "the Sovereign God," or "the God who is more than enough."

After Abram's act of trying to be sufficient within himself, God clearly tells Abram to keep looking to Yahweh for the sufficiency that he needs. God, not Abram, is the All-Sufficient One. God is the God of the Holy Mountain and of the Wilderness. He is the God of the highs and the lows, the good times and the dry times. God is the one who fights for Abram, who has helped him fight kings and enemies and most especially fight for his promises. God is the one who will nourish the promises he gives, who will bring the promise to maturity because he is the Breasted One. God is the Almighty and Sovereign One. God will and can never change from being the God who is more than enough for Abram.

What a reassurance that Abram receives from God. How comforting. This shows God's heart, His character, and this promise and confirmation will sustain Abram through the promise becoming seen in the natural. With this reassuring comfort comes instruction. God tells Abram to live his life in God's presence and be blameless. If Abram lives his life in a conscious way before God as his only audience, then through that intimacy, God will supernaturally empower Abram to live in completeness and wholeness the remaining days of his life.

After all this, God speaks regarding the promise he has given Abram and confirms his covenant with Abram, the promise of descendants and that they will be greatly multiplied! In response to the words of God, Abram has nothing to do but fall on his face in awe before Yahweh. Abram here humbles himself in the dirt and the grace of God flows freely over him.

God continues speaking. He goes on to tell Abram many things. God establishes his covenant with Abram and elaborates on the specifics. Abram will surely become the father of many nations. But now, it is time for a change. Abram must know his new identity to go forward. He must have a new name with a new meaning. God changes his name from Abram to Abraham. With this new name, God continues to repeat promises and expound upon them exclaiming how great and mighty Abraham's descendants will be, how they will be exceedingly blessed, and how kings will come from him. God joyfully expresses how Abraham is indeed to receive the promised land and it will be an everlasting possession to Abraham and his descendants. God covenants to be the God of Abraham and of his children and his children's children.

An instrumental change happens here which promotes Abraham. He receives a new name. His old name, Abram, means "exalted father." However, Abraham means "father of a multitude".[12] There is a difference and it is significant. Abram is already a father to Ishmael. Exalted means elevated in rank, power, or character." Abram has been blessed, he has been successful, acquired wealth, received recognition and power. However, this does not necessarily mean he will be a father of nations. He needs a step up or transformation of his identity.

One of my favorite verses is Isaiah 55:11 AMP, "So will My word be which goes out of My mouth; It will not return to Me void (useless, without result), Without accomplishing what I desire, and without succeeding *in the matter* for which I sent it." Speaking a name over someone is prophesying the meaning of that name over that person. Until this point, when someone called Abram, they were really calling him "exalted father." This of course, came to pass. Ishmael was born and Abram was exalted. However, to catapult Abram into God's destiny for his life, he needed a new name. Instead of people calling him "exalted father," he needed to be called "father of a multitude!" As we have seen the meaning of "Abram" come to pass in his life, now we are sure to see the meaning of "Abraham" become reality as well!

There is something that rises to the forefront in this encounter. God says several times that He is confirming His covenant with Abraham, that He is establishing His covenant with Abraham, and then proceeds to lay out the terms of the covenant. Abraham has a part in the covenant which is to obey its terms. First of all, the covenant is spoken by God in Genesis 17:7 TPT where God says, "Yes, I will establish my eternal covenant of love between me and you, and it will extend to your descendants throughout their generations." What a good God to establish a covenant of love with Abraham and his descendants. This is the nature of God and the very character of God. I John 4:8 AMP assures us that, "The one who does not love has not become acquainted with God [does not and never did know Him], for God is love. [He is the originator of love, and it is an enduring attribute of His nature.]"

I want to differentiate here between two kinds of agreements. There are covenants and contracts. It is especially important to know that God made a covenant with Abraham and not a contract. Without getting too detailed, one of the main differences is that the covenant showed the nature and character of God. A contract is an agreement between parties where each has rights and obligations. If one party does not fulfill their obligation, then they are in breach of the contract and the other party does not have to follow through anymore. However, a covenant is different. Each party has rights and obligations, but here, if one party does not fulfill their end of the bargain, the other party still promises to hold up their end of the agreement regardless of the follow-through of the other party.

Here, God selects the form of the agreement to be a covenant. God is expressing to Abraham that even if he messes up, God will still be faithful and uphold his promises! What a good and faithful God!

As evidence of the covenant, God told Abraham that there would be a sign. This sign would be circumcision. Every male, whether they were born as descendants of Abraham or if they were born into Abraham's household or if they were purchased must be circumcised. Ones born must be circumcised on their 8th day.

The Hebrew word for circumcision is *muwl* which means "to cut short," "curtail," "to blunt," "to cut off," or "to destroy."[13] This obviously is an external sign with sets those who are circumcised apart from those who are not. It is something that clearly marks those people of the covenant. The question that I have had until writing this is "Why circumcision?" I understood that a covenant is marked with the shedding of blood and that obviously happens when one is circumcised. Also, I understand the idea that circumcision cuts off flesh. However, it was not until this morning that I actually received revelation regarding the answer to my own question.

We saw that prior to this encounter, the written account of what preceeds this is that Sarai came up with a Plan B to help the promise come about. We discussed that Sarai said to Abram the following words: "Perhaps through her (meaning Hagar) I can build you a family. Abram listened and did what Sarai asked" (Genesis 16:2 TPT).

It is obvious in looking at the words Sarai spoke that she was trying to build Abram a family and this is clearly expressed in her words "Perhaps through her I can build". We see Abram listened and obediently did what his wife asked. This is a marked indication that the flesh was at work in Sarai's heart and Abram consented to this fleshly scheme. What resulted was Ishmael. Ishmael was the Plan B, not the Plan A of what God had in mind for Abram. Ishmael represents the flesh. However, as we will see, Isaac is God's plan and promise for Abram. I believe, because of this heart of flesh instead of a heart of God, we see the long silence of God for 13 years in Abram's life.

When God does speak with Abram, he speaks of this covenant of love that will be marked by circumcision. I believe that circumcision not only allows for blood to be cut, but it does more symbolically and spiritually. The problem has been, at last evidence, the act of Abram in his flesh. God wants Abram, now known as Abraham, to cut off the fleshly way of thinking and move into the heart and mind of God. It is no coincidence that God chose circumcision to cut off the foreskin of the very intimate part of the body which is capable of reproducing or what we want to think of here as producing the promised child.

Isaac would be conceived through the covenant of circumcision. Abraham's seed would pass through the sign of the covenant and would be conceived not of the flesh but of the promise of God.

This all points to Jesus and we see in Philippians 3:3 TPT that "For we have already experienced 'heart-circumcision'… We are those who boast in what Jesus Christ has done, and not in what we can accomplish in our own strength". The goal is not a physical act of circumcision to cut off physical flesh, but the ultimate root of any physical issues which begins in the heart. Sarai had extra flesh in her heart that needed to be cut off. Any amount of physical cutting will not necessarily mean that the heart has been circumcised. This can only be done by filling your heart with Jesus and cutting all else off. Then the truth of heart-circumcision will be accomplished, cutting away all rights to ourselves, to our schemes and the sins of our flesh, but fully dedicating our hearts to God.

All newborn boys were to be circumcised on their eighth day. Here

God is using numbers to symbolically provide revelation to Abraham. The number eight means new beginnings, superabundant and satiating, abounding in strength resurrection, regeneration, and eternity, and circumcision of the heart.[14] It is interesting that this points to a new day for Abraham, a new era when his promised son will be conceived and be born, and the fulness of the promise to his descendants. The eighth day marks a new beginning of the week, and it will be the start of the birth of the promise for Abraham.

We have seen transformation in Abraham and the prophetic significance of his new name. Now it is time for Sarai to be given a new identity as well. God tells Abraham that Sarai is now to be called Sarah. Before, the name change, Sarai was called "my princess." Now, she was still called "my princess" but with a spelling variation in her name. So, Sarah still means "my princess," but collectively with the new name for Abraham and Sarah, God is telling them that their season of waiting is over. They are entering into a new era. Their names are changed. They are entering their season of promise and destiny.

God assures Abraham here that it is not through Hagar that the promised child will be born, but through Sarah. Sarah will become a mother of nations. Kings will arise from her children and she will be blessed greatly. The Plan A is about to come forth!

Abraham's response is actually very comical, but realistic, considering the fact that he is 99 years old, and Sarah is 89. The Passion Translation is humorous to read because it says that "then Abraham laughed so hard he fell to the ground" (Genesis 17:17 TPT). This would be an awesome scene to watch in a movie about Abraham. Laughter can mean a lot of things. Some people laugh when they are nervous, some when they are feeling other emotions. Laughter does not always mean that their response is to something funny. Here, I think it is a combination of emotions. Abraham does believe God, but this promise seems so unrealistic in the face of his faith. Abraham has been waiting 24 years since God first spoke to him and he has gone on the journey of a lifetime. Abraham, I believe, is overjoyed at the promise of God, anxious about his age and the possibility of this becoming a reality, and it is really far-fetched to think of a woman who is 89 years old walking around blossoming with pregnancy and giving birth to a baby. Sarah could have been a great-great-great-grandmother by this point in her life! Yet, she is having her first baby! God does have a sense of humor.

Abraham sensibly asked God if he would bless Ishmael as his son. But God told Abraham to listen to Him! Open your ears and listen to the words of Yahweh! Stop speaking nonsense about blessing your Plan B!

God promised Abraham that Sarah would conceive a baby and his name would be called Isaac and that his covenant will be with Isaac and his seed. God will bless Ishmael because he is the son of Abraham, but the promise is through Isaac. Then God gave Abraham a timeline of one year. When this time next year comes, Sarah is to give birth to the Plan A, Isaac.

Isaac means "he laughs" or "he (God) laughs".[15] I think that God was laughing with Abraham when he fell to the ground. God was so happy to be the God of Abraham and to be the God of Abraham's descendants and to fulfill this promise in Abraham's life. God was in covenant with Abraham and would fulfill this crazy, unrealistic promise to Abraham despite the circumstances! When God finished speaking to Abraham, he ascended to heaven. He had come down to meet Abraham in his situation to personally bring him the good news of the coming promise, make his covenant of love with Abraham, and to just be with him.

Abraham's response to this God of Love was to obey immediately and without delay. Over and over, we see Abraham hear the instruction of the Lord and obey immediately. That same day, he circumcised himself, Ishmael, and every male of his household. He obeyed immediately, accurately, and thoroughly. Abraham obeys his part of the covenant. He has cut off flesh that so desperately needs to be a thing of the past, to not impede or distract from the fulness of God. God will be more than enough to Abraham and Abraham has demonstrated his need to live his life in God's presence, blameless, honoring the covenant, and patiently waiting in faith for the promise of God.

Encounter #7

Genesis 18:1-19:29: Promise

Encounter 7.1:

Genesis 18:1-15:

God appeared; suddenly three men stood nearby his tent, and they spoke Abraham's response: as soon as he saw them, he ran to welcome them, he bowed down, said they had honored him with their presence and asked them to stay and rest and to stay for a meal he would prepare.

The three men responded to Abraham: *"Very well...go ahead and do as you have said"* (meaning prepare them a meal).

Abraham's response: He hurried back to Sarah's tent and told Sarah they have three guests. Instructed Sarah to quickly get three measures of flour, knead it, and make bread; Abraham ran to the herd, selected a tender calf, and told his servant to hurry and prepare the calf for his guests. Then he brought the meal and set it before his guests. Abraham stood by them under the tree while they ate.

Three men asked: Where is your wife Sarah?

Abraham responded: Over there – in the tent.

One man: **I will return about this time next year, when your wife Sarah will certainly have a son.** (Sarah overheard this. She was at the tent door not far behind him.)

Sarah's response: Laughed to herself with disbelief and said, "A woman my age – have a baby? After I'm worn out will I now enjoy marital bliss and conceive – and with my aged husband."

God's response to Sarah: He knew Sarah's thoughts and asked Abraham, "Why is Sarah laughing, saying, 'How can a woman my age have a baby? Do you think there is anything too marvelous for Yahweh? **I will appear to you at the appointed time next year and Sarah will have a son!**"

Sarah's response: She was afraid and denied saying she wasn't laughing

God's response to Sarah: Yes you were.

Method of encounter/revelation: God appeared in human form (theophany) with two angels who appeared in human form; God spoke; the angels spoke

Location: While Abraham lived by the oak grove of Mamre; Abraham was inside his tent and then went outside his tent; Sarah was inside her tent.

Encounter 7.2:

Genesis 18:16-33

Three men walked off toward Sodom.

Abraham's response: He walked with them to see them on their way.

God said: "Should I really hide from Abraham what I intend to do? After all, he will become a great and powerful nation, and every nation on earth will be blessed through him. It is true: I have singled him out as my own, so that he will lead his family and household to follow my ways and live by what is right and just. I will fulfill all the promises that I have spoken to him."

God explained to Abraham, *"The outcry for justice against Sodom and Gomorrah is so great and their sin so blatant that I must go down and see if their wicked actions are as great as the outrage that has come to me, and if not, then I will know."*

God's two companions went on toward Sodom.

Abraham's response: He remained there (with the other who was Yahweh).

God's response: He paused before Abraham.

Abraham's response: He came forward to present his case before Yahweh and said, "Are you really going to sweep away the righteous while you judge the wicked? What if you find 50 righteous people in Sodom? Isn't your mercy great enough to forgive? Why judge the entire city at the cost of 50 righteous who live there? That's not the one you are – one who would slay the righteous with the wicked – treating them both the same way! Wouldn't the Merciful Judge of all the earth always do what is right?

God's response: **Alright. If I find 50 righteous in Sodom, I will spare the city for their sake.**

Abraham's response: I am just a man formed from earth's dust and ashes but allow me to be so bold as to ask you, my Lord, "What if there are only 5 lacking, and you only find 45 righteous in Sodom? It's not who you are to destroy the entire city for lack of 5 righteous people.

God's response: Alright. If I find 45 righteous in Sodom, I will spare the whole city.

Abraham response: **But what if there are only 40?**

God's response: **Alright. If I only find 40 I will spare the city.**

Abraham's response: He paused. Then said, "Lord, please don't be offended with me, and let me speak… What if there are only 30?

God's response: **Alright. If I find only 30, I will spare the city.**

Abraham's response: Allow me to dare speak this way to you, my Lord. But what if you find there only 20 righteous?

God's response: **Alright. For the sake of the 20 I will not destroy the city.**

Abraham's response: Took a deep breath and asked, "Once more, please don't let my Lord be angry with me if I make but one more request. What if you find only 10 righteous?

God's response: **Alright. I will extend my mercy and not destroy the city for the sake of 10 righteous. God finished speaking with Abraham. He immediately went on his way.**

Abraham's response: Returned home.

Method of encounter/revelation: God appeared in human form (theophany) with two angels who appeared in human form; God spoke and walked with Abraham; the angels walked with Abraham

Location: While Abraham lived by the oak grove of Mamre; walking from his tent area toward the overlook of the plains of the cities of Sodom and Gomorrah.

Encounter but not with Abraham: Two angels (who had previously been with God and Abraham) visits Lot and his family – 19:1-22

Encounter 7.3:

Genesis 19:23-29

God destroyed the cities of Sodom and Gomorrah completely and all the inhabitants and God's fire from heaven fell upon the cities. So, before God destroyed the cities of the plain where Lot had settled, he remembered his affection for Abraham and spared Lot from all the destruction.

Abraham's response: That morning, Abraham hurried back to the place where he had stood before Yahweh. Looking down toward all the land of the plain, he saw columns of smoke billowing up from Sodom and Gomorrah – like the smoke of a furnace!

> Location: While Abraham lived by the oak grove of Mamre; The same place where he had stood before Yahweh at the end of their walk in Encounter 7.2 (overlooking the plain of Sodom and Gomorrah).

While Abraham lived by the oak grove of Mamre, he had Encounter number 7. The meaning of Mamre is significant as to the location of this encounter. "Mamre" means to be strong, to be bitter, or to change.[16] I believe these words are linked to provide us a more thorough status of Abraham's journey at this point. Abraham has been waiting for 24 years for his promise to be realized. He has gone on a faith journey with God, blindly believing in something he cannot see. He has suffered all ranges of human emotion, I'm sure. Sarah has indeed suffered as well including the shame of being barren, being taunted by Hagar when she conceived Ishmael, a son for Abraham that Sarah could not give him. There were times of bitterness in this faith journey. However, strength came from the intimacy of Abraham's relationship with God and this has resulted in change. Abraham has obeyed all the instructions of the Lord. Some of these instructions included major change. Abraham was brought from the city of Ur, some 500 miles from where he is at this point, has allowed his nephew Lot to separate from him, has fought kings to rescue Lot, and has undergone some probably painful physical obedience of circumcision to meet his obligations of the covenant. There have been lots of change. But change is good when it is where God is taking you. And in Abraham's life, he must make change to get to where God can manifest his promise.

Abraham was sitting in the door of his tent during the hottest part of the day and he looked up and suddenly saw three men standing nearby. Looking up is a frequent pattern in Abraham's encounters. It signifies looking toward God, to God's heart, instead of at ourselves or our surroundings to see what is in the natural or visibly before us. Abraham had to look up to see the night sky and the countless stars to get a vision of the magnitude of his descendants. Here he is looking up and God appears with two angels, all three of them in human form. I believe it is clear that it was Yahweh who was appearing to Abraham in human form from the context of Genesis 18:3. Abraham bowed down to worship and called one "My Lord" which is the word for *'adonai* or Lord which is used over five hundred times in the Bible for God.[17] We will see in Genesis 19:1 that the other two men were the two angels that visited Sodom.

Abraham ran to the men as soon as he saw them to welcome them. Abraham was quick to welcome the presence of God and to recognize the identity of his visitors. Abraham bowed down, most likely in worship, and passionately requested that his visitors stay, having honored him with their presence. Abraham asked them to stay for a while, not just for the moment. Abraham wanted time with God, to visit with Him, to share of his best meal and drink, and to allow him to wash His feet. Abraham was so excited that the Lord had come to his dwelling place, his tent, his place of abode, to be with him.

But Abraham had to leave his tent to go to them. Abraham could not stay inside his tent, even at the door of his tent. He had to leave what was comfortable to him, even in the hottest part of the day, and go outside where it was even hotter, to be in the intimate presence of God. There was no debating about this at all. Abraham ran to them instead of continuing to rest at the door of his tent.

The tent, as we have discussed before, represents one's body, the limitations of oneself or thought or even faith. Abraham knew he had to leave his own boundaries and run to the endless possibilities found with his God, the one with whom he now has a covenant of love.

With their consent, Abraham hurries to tell Sarah that they have guests, and she is to make an extravagant amount of bread. Then Abraham ran to his herd and selected a choice calf and instructed his servant to prepare it for his guests, along with other delicious food for them. When this meal was prepared, Abraham set it before the men and stood by them under the tree while they ate.

Instead of making just enough for his guests, Abraham prepared an elaborate feast for them. He did not give to God less than what he should have, or just enough, but way more than was required. This is a testament to the heart of Abraham and his willingness to give to the Lord. He blessed the Lord and gave him of his best and out of abundance.

The visitors asked Abraham where Sarah, his wife, was. Abraham told them that she was in the tent. In the dialogue between Abraham and the men, Abraham has never told them that he has a wife or that her name is Sarah. They knew this information already and this question of where she was is not really a question, but more of a statement showing Abraham that they have revelation knowledge about Abraham and his wife.

Then God spoke these words to Abraham: "I will return about this time next year, when your wife Sarah will certainly have a son" (Genesis 18:10 TPT). God tells Abraham about a future encounter one year out where God will return and visit Sarah and she will certainly have a baby. Sarah was listening and heard all this. Note that Sarah was still at the tent door, not outside her tent. Sarah responded by laughing at these words. The scripture does say she laughed "with disbelief" at the thought of this happening. Her heart was filled with the facts of the situation. She considered her old age, her barrenness, and the impossibility of marital bliss she would enjoy if this were true. Sarah was still in the confines of her limitations and her reaction and words reflected the true nature of what filled her heart.

However, Yahweh knew her thoughts. He did not speak to Sarah, but to Abraham. He asked why Sarah was laughing. He asked Abraham, "Do you think there is anything too marvelous for Yahweh" (Genesis 18:14 TPT)? Jeremiah, almost 3,000 years later answered this question saying "There is nothing too hard for you" (Jeremiah 32:17 TPT). The word "marvelous" as used in verse 14 here is the same Hebrew word that is used as a title of Jesus in Isaiah 9:6 which is "Wonderful." There is nothing too wonderful for God because He is Wonderful. He wants to not only promise and fulfill his promise to Abraham, but do it in such a way that shows off his ability to far surpass and exceed his expectations. "*Never doubt* God's mighty power to work in you and accomplish all this. He will achieve infinitely more than your greatest request, your most unbelievable dream, and exceed your wildest expectation! He will outdo them all, for his miraculous power constantly energizes you." (Ephesians 3:20 TPT)

God repeats what he has just promised. He confirms that he will appear at the appointed time in one year and Sarah will have a son! Sarah became afraid because of how she had responded and denied her heart and her words. But, the Lord knew her heart and told her she had said those words of doubt.

Their time has come to an end at this location and the three men began to depart, walking toward the city of Sodom. Abraham did not just bid them farewell. He wanted to stay with the Lord and he walked with them as they neared the overlook of the plain of Sodom. As they were walking, God spoke to Abraham again.

As we walk with the Lord in our journey, He will speak to us. This happened with Abraham and brought about something that we have not seen to this point in Abraham. The conversation they have shows us that God was walking with and talking Abraham through intercession for other people. We see this later in Abraham's prayer to spare the life of Abimelech and to open the wombs of his wife and servants. One powerful component to Abraham's growth and in his role as prophet is his ability to intercede in prayer for others.

As Abraham was walking with Yahweh, I imagine they were side by side. God knows where he is headed and has not revealed this to Abraham. God is going to see the face of Sodom, to judge the city and its people for their wickedness because the cries of laments and cries of abuse and wickedness for justice had risen to God. The nature and character is one of mercy and justice and grace. I believe that because of God's covenant of love with Abraham, He wanted to share what he was about to do and in intimacy talk about this with Abraham. God says that he has singled out Abraham as His own and Abraham will lead his family and household in the ways of the Lord. This is the first reference to the ways of Yahweh. God's ways should be our ways. If we are living in intimacy with God, those ways will align and be God's ways. This is one powerful key regarding intercession. Abraham is about to intercede for the people of Sodom and Gomorrah.

We will see Abraham appealing to Yahweh to do only what God can do that is within his nature and character. Abraham asks God to do what God does – to Be Himself – to Be Mercy – to Be Justice!

Abraham knew the character of God, his attributes, and the ways of God. God cannot do anything that is out of his character. So, prophetically speaking, Abraham spoke the character of God to God and asked that God act in accordance with Himself on behalf of the people.

God explains to Abraham that he must see if the wickedness is as serious as the outcry is from the city. He must judge the wickedness. At this point, the two men (angels) go on toward the city leaving Abraham alone with God. Here they have their most intimate conversation or intercession. Abraham spoke to God as Judge and again (we have seen this before) Abraham presents the case of the people to Him.

Abraham asks if God is really going to destroy all the people of the city, even if there are fifty righteous ones there. Abraham petitions God to grant the people mercy and forgiveness if there are fifty righteous ones found. Abraham expresses to God his own nature and character which is Merciful Judge! Yahweh tells Abraham that He will spare the city if fifty righteous are found.

Prophetically speaking, the number fifty is significant, and this is the number of people Abraham starts with in his intercession for mercy. Fifty represents jubilee, liberty or liberation, release and freedom, deliverance and rest, and extreme grace. By God's consent to Abraham's request of finding fifty righteous people, He is declaring that He is the God of liberty, freedom, deliverance, and extreme grace! God will act within his character and as judge he will and can only be Merciful Judge!

Abraham then goes on to ask for the same mercy for 45 people, for 40 people, for 30, 20, and finally 10 righteous people. Each time, Merciful Judge consents to Abraham's request for mercy and grace for the people.

Abraham's etiquette and diplomacy were constant and brought about favor and merciful response each time. Abraham was respectful, honoring, yet came boldly to present his case. Hebrews 4:16 KJV tells us, "Let us therefore come boldly unto the throne of grace, that we may obtain mercy, and find grace to help in time of need." Abraham did this, boldly petitioning Merciful Judge who sits on the throne of grace.

Abraham ends with the request for the city to be spared if only ten righteous are found. Abraham could have gone to a lower number, such as 3 or 1, but he stopped at 10. The number ten is significant and has some insightful meaning to glean from here. Ten means complete, or completion of order or cycle, and full. For example, there are ten fingers. With ten fingers, you can carry out in an orderly way what you set your hands to do. It signifies order and completeness. If ten people were found who were righteous, God would spare the city. This signifies a completeness, an orderliness in the justice of God. God is a God of order and He does not do anything out of chaos. Also, ten here, I believe points us to how the heart of God is to have the city dwell and operate out of order and completeness, not out of chaos and disorder which was what was going on resulting in the cries for justice. Lastly, Abraham knew that ten was the number of his relatives who lived there which included Lot, his wife, their children and future spouses. Abraham is interceding for the entire city but stops knowing he has interceded for his beloved nephew and family to be spared.

After Abraham requested that the city be spared for the sake of ten righteous people, Yahweh answered and said, "Alright. I will extend my mercy and not destroy the city for the sake of ten righteous" (Genesis 18:32 TPT). Abraham was successful in his intercession and in his case before Yahweh, presenting his case face to face with Merciful Judge, intimately, respectfully, boldly, and victoriously.

Then Yahweh went on his way toward the city of Sodom to take care of justice but remembering his affection and the covenant of love He had made with Abraham. Abraham returned home.

What we learn is that the two angels entered the city of Sodom. They met Lot and the result of their interactions is that the angels plead with Lot to leave the city and to take his family because they are going to destroy the entire city and its inhabitants. The city is so full of wickedness. The men of the city even try to take the angels and sexually violate them. Whereas Abraham has a covenant of love with Yahweh and has grown in his relationship with the Lord intimately and purely, the opposite is happening in Sodom. Intimacy is being abused and twisted and deviation from everything pure and true is rampant.

So, Lot and his family leave Sodom. The next morning, Abraham hurried back to the same place where he had stood face to face with Yahweh and pleaded his case, looking down on the plain of Sodom and Gomorrah. As he stood there, he saw the massive columns of smoke that burned like a furnace and rose into the heavens. Abraham saw with his eyes the destruction. A beautiful reference is found in Genesis 19:29 TPT regarding God's judgment. It says, "So before God destroyed the cities of the plain where Lot had settled, he remembered his affection for Abraham and spared Lot from all the destruction".

This reminds me of the story of Joseph, Abraham's great grandson. Joseph had been despised and hated by his brothers, thrown into a deep pit to die, but then sold into slavery. After Joseph was sold into slavery, he, through a series of divinely miraculous events, became the master of Potiphar's house. Potiphar was officer of the Egyptian Pharaoh. Genesis 39:5 TPT tells us that "Yahweh blessed the Egyptian's affairs for Joseph's sake". God did this again when Joseph became the Head of Agriculture for Pharaoh. God blessed everything that Joseph put his hands to and God blessed those around him for Joseph's sake. God loved Abraham and because of God's love for Abraham, he spared Lot, for Abraham's sake. God surely did not forget Abraham in his acts of judgment. He remembered him and his love and affection for Abraham. It was because of God's love for Abraham, and for Abraham's sake that He spared Abraham's nephew Lot.

Encounter #8 (with Sarah)

Genesis 21:1-7: Promise

Yahweh visited Sarah, just as he said he would, and fulfilled his promise to her.

> And Sarah conceived and bore Abraham a son in his old age, at the exact time God had promised them.
>
> Abraham's response: Named his son Isaac, the miracle son. When Isaac was 8 days old, as God had commanded him, Abraham circumcised Isaac. Abraham was 100 years old.
>
> Sarah's response: Spoke, "God has brought me laughter and everyone who hears about this will laugh with me. Who would ever have told Abraham that Sarah would one day nurse children! Even though Abraham is an old man, look – I have given him a son!
>
> Method of encounter/revelation: God visited Sarah (perhaps in a dream, perhaps physically)
>
> Location: last known location was southern region of Canaan between Kadesh and Shur in a place called Gerar (however, King Abimelech told Abraham he was free to settle wherever he pleased after the release of Sarah – Genesis 20:15); Abraham could have journeyed back to the oaks of Mamre (where he had come from) because in Genesis 20:1 it indicates that Abraham's intentions were only to live as a temporary resident in Gerar.

This is a special encounter because it is with Abraham's wife, Sarah. Because Sarah is Abraham's primary wife, I include this encounter as it relates to Abraham. Being that they are married, there is unity and oneness. Therefore, including this encounter, I believe is necessary. As a note, there was a previous encounter with Hagar in the wilderness. I have chosen not to include that encounter, even though Hagar was a secondary wife to Abraham. I intentionally did not include this as one of the major encounters of Abraham because

Hagar was not the primary spouse and the reasons why she became his wife were due to reasonings of the flesh as a Plan B for Abraham's life.

Yahweh visited Sarah. We aren't sure if it was a physical visitation or if He appeared to Sarah in a vision, but God did visit her. He came to Sarah as he had promised a year earlier when He, along with two angels had visited Abraham outside of his tent. The last promise spoken by God was, "I will appear to you at the appointed time next year and Sarah will have a son" (Genesis 18:14 TPT)! We see that God did just exactly as he said. In fact, that previous encounter, God verbally said two times that he would visit Sarah in a year and that she would conceive a baby. God didn't just make a promise to Abraham and Sarah. He didn't tell them that He would visit Sarah in one year. He didn't just tell them that at the next visit, Sarah would conceive. He didn't just tell them that Sarah would conceive have a son. God did what he promised. God fulfilled every one of the details of the promise. God visited Sarah at the appointed time. Sarah did conceive a baby, and it was a son!

The question that God asked Abraham in the last encounter, "Do you think there is anything too marvelous for Yahweh" (Genesis 18:14 TPT)? begs the answer now. No, there is nothing too marvelous for God. We don't have to wait 3,000 years until Jeremiah, the prophet, answered that question. The answer is shouting out, "No! There is absolutely nothing too hard for Yahweh!" God has done the impossible.

Romans 4:17 AMP says, "**(**as it is written [in Scripture], "I have made you a father of many nations"**)** in the sight of Him in whom he believed, that is, God who gives life to the dead and calls into being that which does not exist." God has spoken promises and prophesied to Abraham about his promised son. Abraham was 75 years when he started on the faith journey. Twenty-five years later, Isaac is born.

The wait was twenty-five years. This is a significant number and teaches us powerful lessons in the faith journey of Abraham waiting and then finally receiving his promised son, Isaac. It means being brought to account by the grace of God, experiencing grace or mercy.[18] Broken down into the different meanings of twenty and five, we see that twenty in itself means expectancy, waiting, accountability, responsibility, and service.[19]

Five means grace, abundance, favor, and redemption.[20] All this tells us the story of Abraham's journey of faith. We see that the majority of his faith walk, there was an expectancy and long years of waiting. However, we see Abraham grow in accountability and responsibility. We see him lead in acts of service, for example when he rescued Lot from the enemy kings. Lastly this series of growth is topped off with abundance of grace and favor leading to redemption. Abraham was brought to account only by God's grace and in spite of his humanity, his faith endured, and God has blessed him with Isaac, the seed of promise which will result in a harvest of descendants too numerous to even count.

In Genesis 17:19, God instructed Abraham that he would name his promised son Isaac. This happened during an encounter that took place one year before Sarah conceived Isaac. Here God is prophetically speaking the promise of delayed laughter being fulfilled because the meaning of Isaac is "delayed laughter".[21] In this previous encounter, Abraham laughed so hard at the thought of Sarah having a baby that he fell to the ground. Abraham is still on the ground when God spoke out loud to him and promised that Sarah would indeed conceive a son and that his name would be "delayed laughter" or Isaac. Here God is giving Abraham the desires of his heart, not only the fact of having a son, but the joys that would go along with that. God would bring laughter to Abraham, even in his old age. The meaning of Isaac can also mean that "he (God) laughs." God is also laughing with Abraham at the impossible promise He has said he will fulfill for Abraham. We will see this laughter change from the result of receiving the impossible to seeing the possible.

Abraham named his miracle son, Isaac. The name "Isaac" in Hebrew is *Yitzhak* and means "he laughed." This is the past tense word for laughter. It is "delayed laughter".[22] When he was born, Sarah said, "God has brought me laughter, and everyone who hears about this will laugh with me" (Genesis 21:6 TPT). This laughter was delayed throughout the faith journey of twenty-five years. But even before this, the lack of a son was evident. Seeing the women Sarai (as she was called back then) knew have their own babies and laugh with joy, to seeing Hagar conceive and give birth to Ishmael, Sarah is now full of her own joyful laughter.

This is a different kind of laughter now. Her laughter has turned from disbelief at the possibility of joy, to complete saturation of the abundance of God's faithfulness to her. Abraham experienced laughter at the last encounter after God promised to wonderfully bless Sarah and that she would have a son and she would become a mother of nations. In fact, Abraham laughed so hard, he fell to the ground. Trying to comprehend the wonderful and abundant promises of God does not work when we only limit them to our own natural understanding. Everything about the promise is ridiculous. Abraham was imagining this ridiculous promise coming to pass, contemplating Sarah at age 90 pregnant and giving birth. Abraham at age 100 would become a father of this promised son. Can you imagine how everyone they knew would react? Abraham's only natural reaction was to fall to the ground laughing at this absurdity.

Now, Sarah, in her joyfulness, says that everyone who hears about this miracle will laugh with her. Laughing is contagious. Especially the laughter which expresses complete joy in knowing that God, who is More than Enough, the Creator of the Universe, the Merciful Judge, and the one who made a covenant of love with

Abraham, has fulfilled his promise to Abraham. His son Isaac has been born and has brought delayed laughter and joy in his old age. God is fulfilling his covenant promises to Abraham. Together, their laughter has turned from the ridiculousness of the promise to the joys of the promise. Even God now laughs with Abraham and Sarah in joyful celebration of the birth of Isaac.

Abraham obeys his part of the covenant and on Isaac's eighth day, Abraham circumcises his son. Isaac was conceived through the covenant, since Abraham was already circumcised. Now Isaac is himself circumcised. He was born of the promise. Now he is set apart and carries the sign of the covenant on his flesh. Abraham has dedicated Isaac to the Lord and reiterated his desire to cut the flesh away and only go after the heart of Yahweh. Eight is the number of new beginnings. There is a newness, a freshness, and a new era ahead.

Encounter #9

Genesis 21:12-14: Promise with instruction

God spoke to Abraham: <u>Don't be distressed over the slave woman and her son. And whatever Sarah says to you, do it</u>, **for it will be through Isaac your promise of descendants will be fulfilled. Rest assured, I will make the son of your slave woman into a nation too, because he is your son.**

Abraham's response: Rose up early the next morning, bundled up food and water, strapped them to Hagar's shoulders; gave her his son and sent them away. (He did what Sarah said)

Method of encounter/revelation: God spoke

> Location: Somewhere near the wilderness of Beersheba (since that is where Hagar and Ishmael wondered off into after Abraham sent them away)

In the last encounter, after twenty-five years of faithful patience, Isaac, the promise was born! Isaac brought joyful and delayed laughter to Abraham, Sarah, God, and all those who heard what God had done!

Here, we are faced with the fruit of the flesh. But, God comes to speak words of instruction to Abraham and words of promise. At this point, Isaac is now weaned. Although we aren't sure of Isaac's age at this point, he is most likely somewhere between the age of two and four. This is the age when he can eat solid food and stop drinking breastmilk from his mother. According to Jewish customs, the time when a child is weaned is a cause for great celebration. The child is now old enough and has successfully completed his infancy stage. Abraham prepared a great feast to celebrate.

There was much to celebrate. The joy of now having Isaac, this precious gift who was once a promise, is now a little boy and not a baby anymore. He is growing and maturing and his parents have found wonderful joy in being his parents. Isaac has certainly brought about laughter to his aged, but abundantly happy mother and father. Sarah's pride is her handsome little boy, the one she has given Abraham in his old age, and he is the star of the show. As the celebration intensifies and the party goes on with festive dance, conversation, the best food, and joyful laughter, Sarah is painfully confronted by the harvest she initiated some fifteen-ish years ago.

At that time, Sarai (as was her name then) had born no children. Sarai came up with a way to give Abram (as was his name then) children. She had a strategy. This was a Plan B, a scheme from her heart of flesh. "Sarai said to Abram, 'Please listen. Since Yahweh has kept me childless, go sleep with my maidservant. Perhaps through her

I can build you a family.' Abram listened and did what Sarai asked." (Genesis 16:2 TPT)

Sarai thought that through her strategy, she could have Hagar step in and hopefully conceive and give birth to a child for Abraham. This was not God's strategy. God's plan was Plan A, but here, Sarai was tired of waiting and she was getting much older and she had not seen God's Plan A come to pass. God's Plan A was for Sarai to be the mother of nations and for her to be the mother of the promised child. Sarai's eyes dictated to her heart and she spoke what was in her heart out of her mouth. I'm not sure if Sarai contemplated on what would happen later as a result of Ishmael being born. Did Sarai really believe that she would ever have a baby. This leads me to believe that she did not. If Sarai really believed she would have Isaac, she would never want Ishmael to have been born to supersede Isaac or his intended blessing.

Plan Bs have a way of producing Ishmaels that mock Isaacs. This is exactly what happened. At the celebration of Isaac's weaning, Sarah noticed Ishmael making fun of or threatening her son, Isaac. This could not be tolerated. The fierce and protective motherly pride rose up in Sarah and she had to do something drastic. She had to eliminate the threat of Ishmael to her Isaac.

Sarah told Abraham, "Get rid of this slave woman and her son. Banish them, for the son of that slave woman must not become a coheir with my son Isaac" (Genesis 21:10 TPT)! What Sarai thought was a great strategy has resulted in pain. Even though she now has Isaac, there is also Ishmael, which has resulted in negative consequences.

It is interesting that in her passionate outcry to Abraham, Sarah doesn't call Hagar by her name, but she calls her "that slave woman." Even though Hagar has always been Sarah's maidservant, now this is used negatively against her. When Abram listened to Sarai and took Hagar to be his secondary wife, he was taking someone "in chains" and aligning himself to that status of servanthood. Anything that resulted from that union would be tainted and could never be God's Plan A. Now, the situation has escalated, and something must be done. Sarah has waited for so long to have Isaac and now she has him. He is weaned, but his inheritance is jeopardized by Ishmael. Sarah does not want him to be coheir with her son. She has heard God make repeated promises to Abraham about how He will bless their promised son.

Abraham was obviously upset by the wishes of Sarah to completely banish Hagar, and especially his son Ishmael. Abraham loved Ishmael just as he loved Isaac. Ishmael was no less his son. God spoke to Abraham to eliminate the mental wrestling match going on in Abraham's mind about what to do. God eased Abraham's distress and said, "…whatever Sarah says to you, do it, for it will be through Isaac your promise of descendants will be fulfilled. Rest assured, I will make the son of your slave woman into a nation too, because he is your son" (Genesis 21:13 TPT).

God tells Abraham to do the exact thing that he did when he took Hagar to be his second wife. God tells him to do whatever Sarah tells him to do. He listened and did as Sarai requested the first time. Now, he is to listen and do whatever Sarah says this time as well. Why would God tell Abraham to listen to Sarah and follow her wishes the second time when the first-time lead to this disaster? This time, God is instructing Abraham to follow Sarah's wishes. The first time, Abram just listened and did as Sarai asked. He acted without following the instructions of God.

We can do something that seems so similar yet is so drastically different and which leads to our Plan B or our Plan A. Here, in the outset, Abram only obeyed Sarai's wishes. But later, we see Abraham followed Sarah's wishes and it was instructed by God to do so. There is a major difference.

God assured Abraham that He would still bless Ishmael and make him into a nation just for the reason, that he was also Abraham's son. However, God promised that it would be through Isaac that His promise of descendants would be fulfilled. So, both sons would be blessed and would become nations because of blessing on Abraham. However, the promise would only result through God's Plan A, Isaac!

So, Abraham obeyed God and did as Sarah instructed. He acted immediately beginning his follow through early the next morning. He prepared provision for Hagar and Ishmael of food and water. Then Abraham gave Hagar his son and sent them away. Abraham did not try to keep and salvage the Plan B. He let it go and held on to Plan A. This was really a test for Abraham, the first of two, which would involve him letting go of each of his sons. God promised Abraham that he would be the father of many nations and his descendants would be as numerous as the stars in the skies and the sand on the seashore. Now he has two sons, both born at a very old age. One was the son of flesh, the other the son of promise. However, they were both his sons. Now, Abraham must let go of Ishmael. We have seen a cutting away in Abraham's life with the circumcision required by God as Abraham's part of the covenant. Abraham has dedicated himself to a cutting away of the flesh. Now, he must send away his first son and release him. Abraham must feel an overwhelming sense of pain and even a sense of "what if?" something terrible should happen. What if something terrible should happen to Isaac and then Abraham is again left with no sons? However, Abraham does not voice any such words or doubt. He only obeys and sends Ishmael away.

Ishmael is now no longer a risk or a threat to Isaac. Things seem to be proceeding nicely and going well. Isaac is growing and maturing, and it is through him that the fullness of God's promise rests.

Encounter #10

Genesis 22:1-19: Promise with instruction

God tested Abraham. God said, **"Abraham!"**

Abraham's response: Yes, I am here.

God's response: <u>Please take your son, your only son, Isaac, whom I know you dearly love, and go to the land of Moriah. Offer him up to me as a burnt offering on one of the mountains which I will show you.</u>

Abraham's response: Early the next morning, Abraham cut wood for burnt offering, loaded it on his donkey, set out for the distant place God had shown him, took with him 2 of his servants, and his son Isaac. On the 3rd day, Abraham looked up and saw the place in the distance. Abraham spoke to the servants: Stay here with the donkey. Isaac and I will go up and worship, then we will return to you. Abraham took the wood for the burnt offering, placed it on his son's back. Abraham carried the knife and the fire, the two of them walked up the mountain together.

"Father, we have the wood and the fire, but where is the lamb for the burnt offering?" asked Isaac.

Abraham's response: My son, God himself will provide the lamb for an offering.

They went on together.

When they arrived at the place on Mount Moriah that God had shown him, Abraham built an altar and stacked wood on it. He tied up his son Isaac and laid him on top of the wood on the altar. Then Abraham took the knife in his hand to plunge it into his son, BUT…

God's response: The angel of Yahweh called to Abraham from heaven, saying, "Abraham – Abraham!"

Abraham's response: Yes, I'm here.

God's response: Do not lay a hand on the boy or harm him for now, I know you are fully dedicated to me, since you did not withhold your son, your beloved son, from me.

Abraham's response: Looked up, his eyes fell on a ram caught by its horns in a thicket; Abraham took the ram and sacrificed it as a burnt offering in Isaac's place.

<u>Abraham named the place, "Yahweh appears."</u>

God's response: Yahweh's angel spoke a second time from heaven: "I solemnly promise you, by the glory of my own name, decrees Yahweh, because you have obeyed my voice and did not withhold from me your son – your beloved son, I will greatly bless you! I will make sure your seed becomes as numerous as the stars of heaven and as the sand of the seashore. Your offspring will take possession of the city gates of their enemies. Because you have obeyed me, the entire world will be blessed through your seed".

Abraham's response: Abraham and Isaac returned to the waiting servants, and they departed for Beersheba where Abraham had settled.

> Method of encounter/revelation: God spoke; Yahweh's angel spoke; God appeared by having a ram appear in the thicket.
>
> Location: Beersheba (Philistine country); journey from Beersheba to Mount Moriah; and then back to Beersheba

The last encounter ended with Abraham sending his son, Ishmael, into the wilderness with his mother. This is a test for Abraham in releasing his son, something he waited until old age to see in his life. Here, Abraham obeys God and does as Sarah wishes to banish Ishmael to prevent him from usurping the blessing of Isaac. Ishmael, even though he is not the promised son, is still in fact Abraham's son, and Abraham loves him. Abraham is heartbroken about sending Ishmael off into the wilderness but does not succumb to fleshly desires. Instead, we see Abraham only follow his heart and that is the voice of God.

Now, we find Abraham starkly facing another test, without a doubt the most significant test he will ever face. Abraham has another encounter with God sometime after he sends Ishmael off with Hagar. God spoke with Abraham and gave him these instructions: "Please take your son, your only son, Isaac, whom *I know you* dearly love, and go to the land of Moriah. Offer him up to me as a burnt offering on one of the mountains which I will show you" (Genesis 22:2 TPT).

This narrative in Genesis 22 is referred to as the Akedah, or the Binding of Isaac. It is sometimes called *Akedat Yitzchak*, literally meaning the Binding of Isaac (*Yitzchak* is Isaac). This is the story of how Abraham was tested by God to bind his only and beloved son Isaac and to offer him as a sacrifice to God. Just as Abraham has the knife raised to kill Isaac, he hears the voice of an angel of God speak and instruct him to stop because Abraham's heart is truly known by his complete and unwithheld obedience to God. We see that a ram, just at that moment, is seen in a nearby thicket, which is then substituted for Isaac and becomes the sacrifice.

The Akedah is not only a true historical account of an encounter Abraham had with Yahweh, but we will see that it is also probably the pinnacle arch- type, a foreshadowing of the ultimate sacrifice that our Heavenly Father would give for our benefit. In John 3:16 AMP, we find that "For God so [greatly] loved *and* dearly prized the world, that He [even] gave His [One and] only begotten Son, so that whoever believes *and* trusts in Him [as Savior] shall not perish, but have eternal life".[23]

We see that God's first word in the instruction to Abraham was "Please". God knew just how much that Abraham loved Isaac, how long he had waited for Isaac, the journey of faith that he had traveled. If Abraham's love for Isaac was great, God's love for His own Son far surpassed anything that you or I could ever comprehend. God is so loving and so merciful, that in this test, God knows what He is going to ask of Abraham and the sacrifice it will require. This is evident of His heart by the use of the word "Please".

God tells Abraham that He knows how much Abraham loves his son by specifically saying just that, "whom I know you dearly love" (Genesis 22:2 TPT). This is the first reference to the word "love" in the Bible using the word *ahavah*.[24] Therefore, it is profoundly significant in that it refers to a father's love to a son. This is the ultimate love story so famously expressed in John 3:16 KJV. "For God so loved the world that He gave his only begotten son, that whosoever believeth in him should not perish, but have everlasting life." This is how much God loved the world. He freely gave His only Son, the one He loved with an absolute and never-ending love, all for us!

Even though factually, Abraham has two sons, the instruction here references Abraham's son in the singular, "your son, your only son,

Isaac". As we have seen, Ishmael has been sent away into the wilderness and Abraham has given him up instead of holding on to him. Isaac is now the only son with Abraham. It is clear also that this is in reference to the promise that will come through Isaac and no other. So, for purposes of the promise, Isaac is, in fact, Abraham's only son. This also points to Jesus, who is the only begotten Son of God.

Abraham is to go to the land of Moriah and offer Isaac there as a burnt offering on one of the mountains the Lord will show him. Abraham has grown immensely in his faith walk and here we see perfect obedience to the instruction of God. Abraham did not let one day go by. He acted immediately. Also, there is a Jewish tradition that says Abraham concealed all this from Sarah presumably so that she would not interfere with Abraham's obedience to God's instruction. Abraham wanted to pass the test. He knew what was required. He was a true worshipper of God and knew that he could hold nothing back, including his only beloved son Isaac.

Early the next morning, Abraham got up and cut the wood for the burnt offering, loaded it on his donkey, and set off for Moriah. He took with him Isaac and two servants, so there were four traveling together.

I believe that Abraham, from the moment of receiving these instructions from Yahweh, considered Isaac dead. But his faith was so strong and he was so confident that he knew God would have to resurrect Isaac from the dead. Abraham had seen God work in his life for twenty-five years cause the possible to come from what seemed impossible. Abraham had learned from his act of flesh in producing Ishmael. Abraham was not holding anything or anyone back from the Lord. He was immediately willing to fully obey the Lord.

On the third day, Abraham looked up and saw the place in the distance. The group has been on the journey from Beersheba to the land of Moriah and this is the third day. What we will see is that this is the exact time frame from when Jesus died to when He was resurrected. (We will also see that on the third day Isaac will be resurrected, figuratively speaking.) We have seen that Abraham considered Isaac dead as of when God gave him these orders. Because of Abraham's complete obedience, Isaac was already figuratively dead the moment Abraham surrendered him.

Abraham looked up. He lifted his eyes. This is symbolic that what is coming is very significant. Abraham has looked up before in several instances and we have seen this to be significant. Abraham looked up into the night sky to get a visual of the stars and try and comprehend how numerous his descendants will be. Also, Abraham looked up when he was at the door of his tent and saw the three men, one of whom was Yahweh, and the other two angels in the form of me. So, Abraham, knows the significance of looking up. He is expecting from God, especially now more than ever in this very difficult test which he is so obediently meeting with bold confidence.

Abraham sees Moriah, the place where he is to make the sacrifice. Moriah means "chosen by Yahweh." This word comes from the root meaning "sight," or "vision." So, by reason, Abraham is instructed to go to the mountain of Clear Vision.[25] Abraham walked by faith and not by sight. The sight he received by faith in God was absolutely clear vision.

Abraham instructed the two servants to stay at the bottom of the mountain. He told them, "Isaac and I will go up and worship, then we will return to you" (Genesis 22:5 TPT). Some picture Isaac as being a little boy when this happened, but Isaac was somewhere around the age of 30. He was a grown man.

This is the first instance of worship in the Bible. We see that the context of worship is significant, and it encompasses Abraham freely and willingly giving his only beloved son as a sacrifice to God. This is the definition of worship. Worship always involves sacrifice of self and flesh. In the New Testament, we find that the first reference to worship is when the wise men bow down and present gifts to baby Jesus of gold, frankincense, and myrrh. So, worship involves a bowing down of ourselves, presenting sacrifices and gifts (these are praise to God) to love God by showing him honor and adoration.[26]

Abraham tells the two servants that "we will return to you" (Genesis 22:5 TPT). Abraham was confident that something miraculous would happen. He knew that he and Isaac would return from the mountain. Abraham's faith was so strong that he took this opportunity to think of it as if God had a problem to solve. God has promised Isaac to Abraham as his promised son, the one on whom the promise rests. The promise of descendants as numerous as all the stars in the sky would come from Isaac. So, if God commanded Abraham to sacrifice Isaac, then God would have to restore or resurrect Isaac from the dead. Abraham was absolutely committed to obeying God, so God would have to step in and miraculously fulfill his promise.

Abraham and Isaac walked up the mountain together. The Hebrew says that they both went up in agreement. This is beautiful because it points us to how Jesus was in agreement with the Father. Jesus, when He was in the Garden of Gethsemane and knew the severe test was coming, prayed to His Father, "saying, 'Father, if You are willing, remove this cup [of divine wrath] from Me; yet not My will, but [always] Yours be done'" (Luke 22:42 AMP). Jesus was going up in agreement with His Father, just as Isaac was going up in agreement with Abraham.

Abraham placed the wood on Isaac's back, just as Jesus carried the cross to Golgotha. Abraham carried the knife and the fire, and they both walked up in agreement to the top of Moriah. Isaac saw that they had the wood and the knife and fire, but asked Abraham where the lamb for the sacrifice was.

Abraham's answer prophetically speaks, "My son, God himself will provide the lamb for an offering" (Genesis 22:8 TPT). This answer wasn't a stall on Abraham's part of not telling Isaac that he was the sacrifice intended by God. What Abraham is really saying is that God will provide HIMSELF a lamb for a burnt offering. What a concept! Abraham was so confident in the character and nature and faithfulness of God that he knew God was up to something good.

Abraham and Isaac arrived at the exact spot on Mount Moriah and Abraham began to build the altar and stacking the wood on it. He then tied up or bound Isaac and laid him on the wood of the altar. Abraham then took the knife and began the act of plunging it into Isaac.

But, at that moment, and angel of Yahweh called out to Abraham, "Abraham - Abraham!" Twice, the angel called to Abraham! When someone's name is called out twice, this is for special emphasis! The angel continued to give Abraham a cease-and-desist order not to lay a hand on Isaac and not to kill him. The angel proceeded to say, "for now, I know you are fully dedicated to me, since you did not withhold your son, your beloved son, from me" (Genesis 22:12 TPT).

I can imagine the relief and the realized expectancy Abraham must have felt at hearing those very comforting words. God has seen Abraham's faith, his complete and unwavering faith, his absolute willingness to give back to God what he has spent decades believing for – his only beloved son, Isaac. Can you imagine the faith building this must have accomplished in Isaac as well, knowing well that his father believed for him for twenty-five years, only to see Abraham so intimately ready to thrust a knife into his heart? Isaac has just witnessed ultimate faith, extravagant obedience, and unsurpassed faithfulness of God. What looks impossible is possible. The knife was in action ready to in a moment kill the promised son, but God stopped the knife, prevented death, and substituted a lamb for Isaac. God did provide HIMSELF a lamb for a burnt offering.

Just then, Abraham looked, and his eyes fell upon a ram caught by its horns in a nearby thicket. Abraham took this ram and sacrificed it on Isaac's altar as a burnt offering to God. God presented the substitute for Isaac. It was at this same place, several thousand years later that a lamb would be sacrificed as a substitute for you and me – Jesus Christ, the only begotten son of God.

Abraham named the place "Yahweh provides". Yahweh in his love and faithfulness, did provide a sacrifice. Where God Himself provides for Abraham, God would later provide a Savior for us all.

I believe that Abraham knew that he was pre-acting out what would happen thousands of years later. God is all knowing. He knew that Abraham would be completely obedient and selflessly give Isaac as a sacrifice. Abraham, I believe was so confident in his faith. He was probably around 130 years old at this point. He has believed and seen God do the impossible and believes God will absolutely do it again. Although, I don't believe that Abraham, even though he was a prophet, knew the details about Jesus as our substitute sacrificial lamb, I do believe that he somehow had an idea of what was to come. So, this act wasn't for God's benefit or necessarily for Abraham's benefit. It was for our benefit. We need to see this example of ultimate obedience and have this example to model.

After Abraham named the place "Yahweh provides", the angel of Yahweh spoke to Abraham a second time. The words the angel spoke were confirming words of the greatest comfort, assuring Abraham that because of his obedience and his willingness to not withhold his beloved son, Isaac, from God, the promise God had spoken long ago to greatly bless Abraham and make his seed as numerous as the stars of heaven and the sand of the seashore would surely come to pass. The promise included making sure that the offspring of Abraham would take possession of the city gates of their enemies and that the entire world would be blessed through Isaac.

What a test. It was faith and obedience that brought about the birth of Isaac and it continues to be faith and obedience that Isaac is restored to Abraham. The promise is alive and blessed.

"So Abraham returned unto his young men, and they rose up and went together to Beersheba; and Abraham dwelt at Beersheba." (Genesis 22:19 KJV) Abraham's prophetic words that He and Isaac would return from the mountain to the two waiting servants did come to pass. We know that Isaac did return with Abraham because Isaac's life was figuratively resurrected, and Isaac goes on to live a long life and marry and have children. However, the words in verse 19 are, I believe edited by the Holy Spirit to give us one last look into the beauty of the type we have been examining. Verse 19 says that Abraham returned unto his young men. It does not specifically include Isaac. The person of Isaac is edited out, yet we know that he did come off the mountain alive.

We actually do not have a reference of the person of Isaac written into the scripture until two chapters later when Isaac meets his wife, Rebekah, at the well at Beer-Lahai-Roi, and marries her. I believe that this is significant and points us to the model of Jesus. After Jesus is resurrected, he ascends to heaven. He will be absent from the earth until He returns to meet His bride. Just as the person of Isaac, who typifies the Son, Jesus, is specifically edited out of the text. He is absent from the text, even though he is alive. His name does not appear in the text until Genesis chapter 22 when he returns to meet and marry his bride. Jesus will come for us, his bride – the church, after being in heaven and returns in expectancy of the one He loves![27]

What is even more amazing is that Abraham asks his servant, Eleazar, to go and find a suitable bride for his son, Isaac. Abraham typifies the Father, as we have seen. Isaac points us to Jesus, the Son. The name Eleazar means "Comforter" and is a type of Holy Spirit. Rebekah is of course, the bride. What a beautiful "ending" to a story about the Father of our faith, Abraham. Before he dies, one of his last wishes is for his beloved son, Isaac, to have a bride that is pure and radiant. Just as the Father commissions the Holy Spirit to seek a bride without spot or wrinkle for Jesus, who will come for her.[28]

Only God can encounter Abraham to meet him where he is and help him grow in his walk of faith and obedience yet be so multifaceted in the way he does it. He is so personal to Abraham, yet points us to his only beloved Son, Jesus, in the process. This is Abraham's last recorded encounter before he dies at the ripe old age of one hundred and seventy-five.

Abraham has passed the ultimate test. He has offered everything to Yahweh willingly and without compromise. God has seen his heart. "Abraham's faith made it logical to him that God could raise Isaac from the dead, and symbolically, that's exactly what happened." (Hebrews 11:19 TPT)

This leads us appropriately into Part 2 where we will pull prophetic faith keys from Abraham's life and journey. First, we discover that for Abraham (and it can be so for us) that faith made it logical.

PART 2

CHAPTER 2

Faith Made It Logical

Hebrews 11:19 (TPT) – "Abraham's faith made it logical to him that God could raise Isaac from the dead, and symbolically, that's exactly what happened."

We need to start thinking differently. When we define our methods by the world's standards, we taint our ability to see clearly through eyes of faith. What we put into our minds is what grows. What we put into our hearts and souls is what will begin to flourish. In some ways, there is nothing necessarily wrong about some methods or strategies that the world presents, but it is imperative that we don't start from that point. We must start from the foundation of knowing the voice of God. This is such a key to anything in life.

When we typically think about faith, usually people get the idea that it will all go against normal or worldly logic. We think that God will have us step out in faith and do something that seems so crazy. In essence it is a little nuts when we define faith by traditional thinking. However, what I am trying to emphasize is that if we have transformed our thought life, then whatever God tells us to do is normal. That is the starting point. We don't begin from twisted thinking. We begin from God himself – Truth and Purity Himself. There is no way that can be illogical.

Hebrews 11:6 (TPT) says, "And without faith living within us it would be impossible to please God. For we come to God in faith knowing that he is real and that he rewards the faith of those who passionately seek him." Footnote b says that this means we are powerless to please God, meaning impotent or powerless.

In order to please God, we must have faith in Him. Believing and trusting in Him is crucial. How can we have a relationship with someone without trusting them? We must have faith in order to have a healthy relationship. Otherwise, there are broken dynamics working in the relationship. For example, how can you have a healthy marriage if one person doesn't trust the other person? For the marriage to work, you absolutely have to have trust or by nature, there will a drifting away or even a divorce.

The same is true with our relationship with God. We must put our faith in Him alone. If we don't put 100% of our faith in Him, then we are not fully trusting Him. What He says is Truth. He is not a man that he could ever lie. So, His words are absolute Truth. We can take them to the bank.

God is the creator of us. He knows how we work. He knows what we need. He knows everything we will ever need. He knows everything about us. Just like a manufacturer creates a product and has an instruction manual, God knows how to make us work just perfectly.

When I think about Abraham and his journey of faith, there are so many things that stand out to me. Abraham is called the Father of our Faith. Looking at his life and examining his faith should be something that we all do if we want to better understand the concept of faith and making it a reality.

Put yourself in Abraham's shoes (or sandals). He left his homeland to go to a promised land. He didn't know where he was going, but he went. God told him he was going to be the father of many nations. He had a picture of his descendants as numerous as the stars in the sky and the sand on the seashore. The number of descendants promised to Abraham is staggering. HOWEVER, he was old and Sarah was old. Sarah was too old to have children and they had NONE. Abraham waited for decades for even one child.

During all this waiting we went from being old to being really old. Do you get the picture? Abraham was a real man, not just a character from a story.

Finally, Abraham and Sarah receive the promise of a son – Isaac. It is though Isaac that these descendants will come. Isaac is the prize. He is the gift. He is the initial part of the promise. He is crucial to having descendants. But…God told Abraham to sacrifice Isaac. What? How can this be? Isaac was the promised child. How can there be descendants as numerous as the stars in the sky and as the sand on the seashore if Isaac is sacrificed?

(Human logic…) Isaac didn't have any children of his own yet. Could Abraham and Sarah have more children? These are strategies that would start to brew in the human mind.

The amazing thing is that Abraham obeyed. He was WILLING to obey. If we can stay away from letting the story be so familiar to us that we don't think about Abraham's humanity, we will gain insight here! Abraham was just a man. Yet, in the face of what seemed to take away the promise, he STILL OBEYED!

This is the point in the story where a majority of people would have fallen off the cliff of faith. But faith is faith. Abraham was committed. He had settled the issue of trusting God. He knew God was his source of everything. This is powerful!

As Abraham was ready to bring the axe down on Isaac, a ram appeared just at the right MOMENT! God's timing is always perfect. Allowing our faith in God to work with God's perfect timing creates immaculate circumstances.

We know that the ram was then used as the sacrifice and Isaac was not killed on the altar. If Abraham had gotten the advice of his friends, I can only imagine what advice he would have heard. If Abraham had gotten the advice of the professionals of that day, I can almost tell you it would have been contrary to obeying God.

All the advice from Abraham's friends and circle of advisors would have been what the world would have called "good advice" from caring friends and professionals who mean no harm but are just advising from a different starting point. That advice is not founded on knowing the voice of God.

Psalm 101:6 (TPT) says, "My innermost circle will only be those whom I know are pure and godly. They will be the only ones I allow to minister to me." If we have the desire to get advice from other people, we should be making absolutely sure they are pure and godly. Even then, we need to go back to knowing the voice of God. That is our baseline. That is our lifeline.

So, Abraham knew God's voice. He trusted God absolutely. Abraham had transformed his thoughts from a lifetime of being with God, trusting God, and living by faith. He pushed aside the world's baseline for what is logical and ushered in obeying the voice of God as the gold standard for what is logical. You can't have faith in just anything or anyone. The faith I am speaking of is absolute faith in God. When we absolutely commit ourselves to LIVING BY FAITH in God alone, we transform our thoughts. When we pour the word and voice of God into our lives, that will flourish and grow. Faith becomes the logical thing when it is the thing that is continually sown into our lives and grows. Faith becomes the lifeline to the promises – the only way to do it! When this is the garden of our life, then we can say, like Abraham, that **FAITH MADE IT LOGICAL.**

CHAPTER 3

First Healing – Open Wombs before Sarah Conceived

Abraham is called the Father of our Faith. When we think about this man, we think of his faith in God, in the promises of God to him, and of his faithful life as a mere man to believe and receive what God said. He is called Faithful Abraham for good reason.

One of the very first things we learn about Abram, as he was first called, is that God told him to leave it all behind. This included his land, people, and household and go to a land God would show him. After obeying God and leaving all this behind, we learn that God promised Abram that he would give his seed, his descendants, the land where God had taken him.

At this point, Abram is well advanced in age and over 75 years old. Abram does not have any children. Sarai, his wife, is about 10 years younger than Abram, so she is about 65 years old. However, God has just promised Abram's seed this land, which we call the Promised Land!

Let us fast forward 15 years. Abram's name is now Abraham (we will discuss this in a later chapter). Abraham and Sarah (her name has been changed as well) have journeyed to a southern part of the region of Canaan to live temporarily in a place called Gerar. Gerar was a Philistine city-kingdom

south of Gaza. This is a foreign territory for Abraham and Sarah. Abraham was afraid that the men, specifically King Abimelech, would kill Abraham to take Sarah as his wife. So, Abraham told

Sarah to say that she was his sister and not his wife.

King Abimelech took Sarah into his harem thinking she was just Abraham's sister. One night, Abimelech had a dream. In this dream, God told him that he was a dead man because he had taken Sarah, a married woman, into his harem. Fortunately, Abimelech had not violated Sarah in any way. God did acknowledge to Abimelech that he had taken Sarah with a clean conscience, but that he must release her at once to Abraham. God told Abimelech that Abraham would pray for him and his household and their lives would be spared.

Since Abimelech had taken Sarah into his harem, a curse had come upon the household of Abimelech including his wife and all the female servants. They had become barren and not able to conceive children. Their wombs had been closed.

It is not a coincidence that at this point in Abraham's life, he had been believing for his own promised child, a son, that God had spoken to him about 15 years before. Abraham is now about 99 years old and Sarah is about 89 years old. He is still believing for his own child. Abraham is not getting younger and Sarah is not getting younger. When Abraham received the promise of a child, he was already very old and Sarah was decades past being able to conceive and have children. When it looked completely impossible, even at the very beginning of this promise, time and continually increasing age had only proven to exaggerate the natural circumstances which would defy that promise.

But, Abraham did something remarkable. He looked outside of himself and his own desires and his own wishes and even his own belief in God's promise for himself. He prayed for the VERY THING that he needed, that he had been believing for, that he desperately longed for…for God to open the womb. However, he did not pray this for himself and Sarah, but for the King of the enemy. The King of the Philistines. The King of the place where he was living as a foreigner. Abraham prayed for God to open the wombs of Abimelech's wife and all his female servants. All the while Abraham is praying for others, even what was and could have been his lethal enemy, can you imagine Sarah watching and listening to Abraham's prayer for this very thing she had wrestled with to happen for others?

When Sarah had been taken into the harem of Abimelech, he or one of his men could easily have taken Sarah as a wife. They could have taken the wife that Abraham knew was to be the mother of his promised child.

But here we find something worth noting. Abraham prayed to God to heal Abimelech, his wife, and their female servants. When Abraham prayed, they became fertile again. Abimelech's wife, household, and people began to have babies again.

This is the first healing mentioned in the Bible. When something is mentioned first, we refer to it as the Law of First Mention. This is significant and sets a precedent and standard for that thing. What this means is that the first time a word, idea, or doctrine is used in Scripture, we can examine its meaning which will help us to understand and interpret that word, idea, or doctrine in future references.

Here we find the first mention of healing. A childless man, Abraham, prays for the wombs of Abimelech's people to be opened. This is something that he had not received yet for himself.

This passage describing Abraham praying for Abimelech and his people is at the very end of Genesis chapter 20. It ties in perfectly with the first paragraph of chapter 21. They flow continuously and are seamless. Here we discover that after such a long wait, over 25 years. "Yahweh visited Sarah, just as he said he would, and fulfilled his promise to her. And Sarah conceived and bore Abraham a son in his old age, at the exact time God had promised them. Abraham named his son Isaac, the *miracle* son, whom Sarah bore him." (Gen. 21: 1-3 TPT)

Not only did Abraham receive Isaac by faith when it looked and appeared completely impossible, he prayed for healing and as a result others could receive the same miracle he longed for in his personal life. Abraham was faithful for a very long time, but what brought about the final turnaround for him was his prayer of healing for others. This is such a powerful lesson and key that we learn from Abraham.

Not only did Abraham receive his promised son, Isaac, but Isaac had children and his children had children. Today, we see the fruitfulness of the promise of God to Abraham. Just as he looked at the stars in the sky and the sand on the seashore, we see the millions of descendants of Abraham fulfilling their purpose on the earth today.

A key to your turnaround - to receiving your promise, your miracle - is praying for that same need, that same longing, that same condition to be turned around for someone else – when you haven't received your own promise yet!

Are you like Abraham, waiting for a child of your own? Don't lose heart. Start now and pray for someone else who wants a baby. Do you want to find that person you are to marry? Don't let envy grip you and be jealous of others with good marriages. No! You need to begin to pray for your friends who are also searching for that person they can spend their life with. Do you need a financial miracle? Don't turn bitter and stop giving. You need to immediately begin to ask God to bless those around you for financial blessings. Do you need a physical healing? Don't grow weary. Prioritize others in your prayers and speak healing and wholeness over them.

When you pray for others, you will see that it will open a door for

God to work in your life. I don't believe that it causes God to heal you or grant the blessing. What it does is open your heart. It allows you to give your needs away, to lay them down and not pick them up. Instead, you are lifting someone else up before the Lord and laying yourself down.

There is a saying I hear frequently. It is when your own hands are closed in a tight fist, you can't give, but you also can't receive. When you open your hands to give, they are also opened to receive. The same is true of our hearts and our ability to receive God's promises. Opening our hearts can be done through prayer for others, specifically prayer for something for someone else that you are still believing for yourself.

My success with this principle:

I have experienced the results of this principal working in my own life.

I always knew that I wanted children. I remember when my sister had the first child in our family. I am the oldest and even though I thought I would have children before my sisters, one of my younger sisters had a baby first. I remember just how precious he was. I remember the first time I saw him. I held him and carried him, and I knew I had to give him back to my sister, but I wanted to hold him forever!

When my first child was born, I was so happy. I couldn't believe how precious and beautiful she was. I remember the first time I held her, right after she was born. It was surreal. Comprehending life is incomprehensible anyway, but to hold your own child is incomparable to anything else.

After our third child was born, something that I haven't told many people is that I had a miscarriage. I remember seeing the baby on the ultrasound at my doctor appointment. I wanted more children, so I was very excited and happy. Over the next few weeks, I noticed that something wasn't quite right. When I went back for another doctor visit, my doctor said that I would have a miscarriage. I prayed that this was wrong and that I would be able to keep the baby.

After the miscarriage, I felt disappointed and sad. I had seen the ultrasound. That visual which stayed with me. I knew I still wanted more children. I was in the first part of my 30's when my first child was born. By this time, I had three children and I was older than 35. When you are 35 or older and having a baby, it feels like the doctor treats you as if you were geriatric. I knew I was healthy, and I had faith that I would have another baby. There were a number of months that went by, and I still had no evidence of being pregnant with another baby.

About this time, a very good friend of mine from childhood contacted me. She and her husband never had any biological children of their own. I never asked about it, because I wanted to respect their privacy. A few years earlier, they had adopted a baby girl from China. Now, they were in the process of adopting the second little girl. They had prayed about this and knew that they were to specifically adopt a second Chinese little girl. My friend and her husband are schoolteachers, so they didn't have the financial resources to pay for the expenses of the adoption themselves. They needed to raise about thirty thousand dollars by a certain date. My friend had created a beautiful "flyer" which told about the adoption, the expenses, and the due date for the funds. There was a picture of them with the first little daughter on the flyer. She asked if she could send me a copy.

When I received this information in the mail, at first, I was a little resistant to contribute financially, not because I didn't want to help, but because we had so many expenses of our own. However, as a few weeks passed, I began to think about how I still wanted another baby.

We decided to give a certain amount to our friends to help with the looming adoption expense. As we were giving this amount, I still had no positive results for myself. However, I asked God to bless what we were giving and allow this adoption to go smoothly. I asked God to provide provision for the rest of their expenses. In addition, I asked God for their new baby to be healthy and whole.

About a month after we sowed into our friends for their baby, we found out that we were expecting our own baby number four! I knew that our Asah Coals was a gift and that we received him not coincidentally after we sowed and prayed for our friends for the very thing we wanted.

Job prayed for his friends and the Lord turned his captivity:

The story of Job is one of the more difficult and heart wrenching ones to understand and reconcile in terms of why he suffered so much. The emphasis I want to make is not on why Job suffered, but what ended his suffering.

At the beginning of the Book of Job, we learn some important things about Job. We learn that he was a good man, that he was perfect and upright, feared God and hated evil. He was a man of virtue and towering godly standards. Inferred from Job's impeccable character, he was an honorable businessman and attained his wealth according to wise and honest means.

Job was a very blessed man and had seven sons and three daughters. He had accumulated very impressive substance or in today's terms, his assets and portfolio were extremely sizeable. They included seven thousand sheep, three thousand camels, and five hundred yoke of oxen, and five hundred she asses. He had a very great household. Job chapter 1, verse 3 (KJV) says that "this man was the greatest of all the men in the east."

Life was good for Job. He was enjoying the fruits of his labor and work. The good life came to a violent jolt and changed suddenly.

One day, Job was feasting with his children and enjoying good food and time with his family. They saw someone coming from a distance. This was a messenger and would prove to be the first of four successive messengers that would come that day, each one with news much worse than the one before.

Job was informed that a group of Sabeans had taken all Job's oxen and asses by force, killing all his servants. Only this messenger survived and was fortunate to be able to come and tell Job of this terrible news.

The next messenger arrived while the first was still relating this tragedy to Job. He said that fire had fallen from heaven and burned up all Job's sheep and servants attending those sheep. He alone survived and was able to escape.

While messenger number two was still speaking, a third messenger arrived. When it seemed to be already bad enough, it got worse. He exclaimed that Chaldeans came and took all the camels and killed all the servants with their swords. Again, as with the other messengers, he alone had not been killed.

Lastly, messenger number four arrives with the worst possible news. Job's precious sons and daughters have been killed due to a catastrophic windstorm that destroyed the house, causing it to fall and kill all those inside. This messenger somehow escaped and was the only person who survived.

I can only imagine what Job felt and thought as he heard each messenger come with bad news upon bad news, each growing more devastating. Before one messenger can finish the gut-wrenching news, another arrives with something even worse. Job, a man who loved God and hated evil, a man who had moments before enjoyed the bounty of his success and the good of the world, is now filled with incomprehensible grief. He fell to the ground and tore off his clothes, shaved his head, and worshipped the Lord.

Everything he had worked for had been ruined, lost, and killed. Only Job's wife remained. We don't know the amount of time exactly, but imminently another personal tragedy came forcefully and took Job down further. Satan caused Job to be covered with sore boils from the bottom of his feet to the top of his head. Now, even though Job was still alive, his health had taken a mighty blow. Having lost everything and now his health in agony, he hears from the one person remaining – his wife.

At a time like this, the thing you want to hear from the one person left, the one you love, the one you have covenanted with for life, is to hear wise words of comfort. She took the last jab at Job and let the reigns go with full insult to injury. She questioned his integrity asking if there was a little shred left. This was spoken to Job as more of a statement and not a question, sowing what she believed to be the facts of the situation into Job's spirit. I'm sure that Job was still hoping for something soothing or comforting, but her recommendation was to exclaim that he should curse God and die!

Job is really left with no one. His wife clearly is of no help to him and is full of anger herself at the situation. Her flesh is too real before her and she speaks what is in her heart. We see the character of Job's wife in her reaction and advise to him.

At the worst possible moment in Job's life, when it seems to be the lowest it can ever be, Job still did not sin with his lips.

The news of Job's fortune and blessing savagely lost has spread. Three friends hear of these evil tidings and decide to visit Job to mourn with him in his grief and to comfort him.

These friends try to comfort Job and provide words of wisdom to him. However, we see that they are not purified through the looking glass of heaven. They are soiled with the wisdom of human nature.

Throughout all these conversations with his friends, Job's grief is still ever present, his losses are the focus of conversation, but Job is still inquiring of the Lord. In fact, at one point, the Lord answers Job out of a whirlwind. Job has been living in captivity to the scale of devastation he has suffered. Captivity is confinement and imprisonment. Job has gone from being a man of freedom and successful, joyous bounty to living in the chains of devastation and torment. He is bound by his recent circumstances. Those chains have issued his orders.

We see something poignant. In the misery of Job's current physical and mental state, we see the fresh winds of freedom coming because of what Job is about to do. "And the Lord turned the captivity of Job, when he prayed for his friends: also the Lord gave Job twice as much as he had before." (Job 42:10 KJV)

Job was still in the pit of misery. He had lost his fortune, his children, and his health suffered horribly. In this state, Job prayed for his friends. We do not know the specific prayer he prayed for his friends. However, he prayed for them. I imagine it to be a prayer of general blessing for his friends. In any case, he was not praying for himself at this point. He had turned his heart toward his friends and genuinely and sincerely asked for God's blessings to cover his friends.

This is Job's turning point. The captivity he was subject to would be eliminated. The chains he was burdened with would be broken. The confinement would be liberated. Freedom had come at last to Job. The Lord turned the captivity of Job. This is a breath of fresh air. But the key is the word "when" in verse 10. The word "when" begs the question about what caused the thing to come about. There is a cause-and-effect scenario here. The cause is Job prayed for his friends. The effect is the Lord turned Job's captivity.

This is the same principle had Abraham applied when he prayed for the wombs to be opened for Abimelech and his household. Abraham's wife, Sarah, had not been able to conceive the promised child. Yet, Abraham prayed for children for others.

And then…God allowed Sarah to conceive.

Job was still in the agony of the wake of his disaster, yet he prayed for his friends.

And then…God caused his turnaround.

God not only turned things around for Job, but he gave Job twice as much as he had before. Job's later years were more blessed than his former years.

Job ended up with fourteen thousand sheep, six thousand camels, a thousand yoke of oxen, and a thousand she asses. In addition, he had seven sons and three daughters. Chapter 42 of Job goes on to express that Job's daughters were extremely beautiful and there were none as beautiful as they were.

This principle worked for Abraham, for me, and for Job. God never changes. His principles never change. For emphasis, here is the principle again:

A key to your turnaround - to receiving your promise, your miracle - is praying for that same need, that same longing, that same condition to be turned around for someone else – when you haven't received your own promise yet!

Application:

I am rekindling this principle to burn in areas of my life now. I'm believing for many things to come to pass and for promises to be fulfilled. I have chosen people who are believing for the same things and am praying for them as I would for my own requests.

This principle is really taking a prophecy over your life and engaging in spiritual warfare, praying for others, interceding for others - in this case, by praying for someone else with the same need you have, but haven't received yet.

The Greatest Commandment Sums up the Principle:

Matthew 23:37-40 (KJV) says: *"Jesus said unto him, Thou shalt love the Lord thy God with all thy heart, and with all thy soul, and with all thy mind. This is the first and greatest commandment. And the second is like unto it, Thou shalt love thy neighbor as thyself. On these two commandments hang all the law and the prophets."*

Jesus summed up all the law and the prophets, meaning guidelines and principles we need to prioritize and follow. We need to Love God first and foremost and put him at the top of everything and everyone. Secondly, and flowing naturally from the first, to love our neighbor as ourselves. The principle of praying for the needs of others while you have yet to receive your own promises is in alignment with what Jesus said. When we love our neighbor as we would love ourselves, it must look like something. What does the fruit of that look like? Praying for others when you have needs of your own looks like that kind of fruit. Putting this principle into action is living out the words of Jesus here.

Jesus knew that one result of following these two commandments would be that our own promises would be received. Loving others and praying for them in the face of gaps in our own unrealized promises will cause them to become realized.

Just like Sarah conceived Isaac just after Abraham prayed for the wombs to be opened for Abimelech and his people and…

Just like Job's captivity was turned after he prayed for his friends and… Just like I received my fourth baby after I prayed for my friend…

You too will receive your promise. Find someone to love and genuinely pray for with a need or unfulfilled promise like yours. Commit to pray for that person and rejoice with them in their miracle. You will find that your promise will be conceived and that your captivity will be turned.

CHAPTER 4

Getting rid of a Lot: you don't need everyone with you on your journey

Abraham lived an extraordinary life. He saw the miraculous, the impossible happen proving the word and promise of God to him. However, Abraham didn't start out walking in complete perfection. He was on a journey, as we all are. He learned from his mistakes and God's grace was apparent in his life.

Other than a brief family tree, the first information we learn about Abram (as he was initially called) is the first encounter he had with God. Abraham was in Haran and "Yahweh said to Abram: 'Leave it all behind'" (Genesis 12:1 TPT). These are the first words to Abraham. When God called Abram, these first words are significant. All God's instructions are important and need to be obeyed, but the first ones have a special significance. They will frame the scope of Abram's life and his journey as well as the promise.

Abram's past is somewhat uncertain as far as his personal decisions and lifestyle are concerned. We don't know much about him personally from scripture. However, we do know that, according to tradition, his father, Terah, was an idol maker until his death and the family was from a Chaldean city called Ur. This place was full of idol worship and rampant forms of evil. In fact, *Chaldea* means "demonic" and *Ur* means "flame".

So, Abram's family had been dwelling in a place of demonic flames. This city was located about fifty miles south of Babylon. The Chaldeans were astrologers, idol worshippers, and occultists. The name Ur was named after the moon goddess and this was a center of worship to this entity.[29]

We know that in the very same chapter where we find the first mention of Abram, we read about the people in the same area where Abram's family was from began to build themselves a city and a lofty tower that rose into the heavens. The people there said, "We'll make a name for ourselves, a monument to us" (Genesis 11:4 TPT). An ancient historian, Philo Judaeus, said that each of the workers engraved their own names on the bricks used to build the Tower of Babel to memorialize themselves. Obviously, today we don't know any of their names and they are forgotten to the ruins of history. In seeking to make names for themselves, they engaged in self- worship.[30]

We find out that Yahweh came down and confused their singular language and the people scattered to all parts of the earth. The people could no longer understand each other and so they moved away from each other. Today, we find that there may be close to seven thousand different languages in the world. God confused the languages because the intentions of the hearts of the people were all focused on themselves. God said, "If they have begun this as one people sharing a common language, then nothing they plan to do will be impossible for them" (Genesis 11:6 TPT). When we build without God as the center, it is idolatry. When the creations of man rise to the heavens, but our eyes are not lifted to Our Creator, it is idolatry.

We see that the origins of Abram are from this wicked place, Ur of the Chaldees, where there are flames of the demonic rising to the heavens. We will see later that Abraham (as he was later called), had his eyes on the "heavenly city" (Hebrews 11:14 TPT), whose maker and builder is God.

This is the tale of two cities, one which represents the past, and one which represents the future. God knew that Abram must "leave it all behind" (Genesis 12:1 TPT) because if his heart was still remembering what he left behind, he would find an opportunity to go back. But Abraham, we find, couldn't turn back for his heart was fixed on something far greater, the heavenly realm! (Hebrews 11:14-16 TPT) God took Abraham from an existence of demonic flames to something far greater, a promise of life in a heavenly city.

So, again, the first words of God to Abram are to "leave it all behind" (Genesis 12:1 TPT). God goes on to give some details. Of course, "all" means all, but God does give him three specifics of what to leave, just in case the word "all" is not clear enough. He tells Abram to leave the following three things behind:

1. your native land, and
2. your people, and
3. your father's household. (Genesis 12:1 TPT)

Abram is to leave his native land. Abram is to leave the land of his fathers. We know this is the area near Babylon called Ur of the Chaldees. Also, Abram is currently in a place called Haran, where he has journeyed with his father, Terah. This place is about 600 miles from Ur and is probably located in Turkey. Not only is Abram to physically leave the old land, he is to also abandon the ways, customs, and mindsets of those places. "The Hebrew word *eretz* is etymologically linked to the Canaanite word ratzon, which means 'firmness of will' or 'stubbornness.' God is saying to Abram with double meaning, leave your country but also leave your own will behind in order to enter God's plan. We need to leave it all behind, including our ideas of how God will work."[31]

The current location of where Abram is living is Haran. The meaning of Haran is "parched." As we have seen earlier, the meaning of "Ur" is "flame" and Chaldea is "demonic." It would not take much convincing to leave these places. God has something far greater in mind for Abram than living in a place of demonic flames and a place that is parched. He has a promised land waiting for Abram. This land is fertile and the good of the land overflows with milk and honey.

Abram will need to leave the ways of the native land. In Genesis 18:19, we see that God speaks to Abram and indicates that Abram should hold to and follow the "ways of Yahweh." How different are the ways of the wicked people in Abram's native land compared to the ways of Yahweh. Each of these paths will lead Abram to a different promise. The promise of destruction and disappointment or the promise of life and joyful laughter.

God is calling Abram higher and to himself. By following the ways of Yahweh, Abram will experience tremendous growth in obedience and faith leading to the promise.

The second thing Abram must leave is his people. As we can and should infer, the people of Ur are completely wicked, occultists, and following and choosing evil over righteousness. The culture is perverse, and the mindsets are focused on themselves. They worship idols and gods in the place of the One True God, Yahweh. As a result, the stink of perversity permeates the city, and it is perfumed with the decay of worship and praise to these false gods. God knows that Abram needs to leave these people. He needs to leave these people and separate himself from them.

We know that when someone is moving toward something new and elevated, that person will most likely not achieve the new level if they continue to surround themselves with the same old people, filled with the same old mindsets. We hear that you are the average of the five people you surround yourself with on a constant basis. So, if this is true, Abram surely needed a reset. He needed a change. He needed a new life with new vision.

The third thing Abram must leave is his father's household. Even though there is no specific definition of who is included in his father's household, I believe that this excludes every relative not in his immediate family. Abram was married to Sarai and he had acquired many servants. They did not have children at this point. Therefore, anyone outside of Abram's immediate family, according to God's instructions, should be left behind. We know that Abram had an uncle named Nahor (who was also his father-in-law). We know that Nahor had other children. Also, Abram's deceased uncle, Haran, had a son named Lot, who was Abram's nephew. So these were some of the close relatives of Abram, but they were not in Abram's immediate family.

Sometimes, it is very easy to leave people that we have no specific relationship with such as people of a city or people that just live nearby. However, the more challenging relationships are those of relatives. No matter what, they are still relatives and related by blood. If they are choosing right, this is great, but if they consistently choose evil, this can be very challenging in terms of maintaining a relationship with them. There are so many blatant relationship factors with relatives, but there are also the more subtle nuances that can often be more powerful undertones that bubble to the surface of relationships with these close relatives. Sometimes, there are powerful events that occur but are never spoken about, there are feelings that are never resolved, and so on. However, one of the factors that sway and influence, even if not intentional, are the relationships we have with our family. This is why God instructed Abram to leave even the people of his father's household behind as well. God did not want any distraction for Abram.

After God instructed Abram to leave it all behind, we learn that "Abram obeyed Yahweh and left; and Lot went with him…He took his wife Sarai, his nephew Lot, and all the possessions and people he had acquired in Haran; and they departed for Canaan" (Genesis 12:4-5 TPT). So, Abram left and started on his journey. I believe that Abram would have had less obstacles to overcome on his journey of faith if he had fully complied with leaving exactly what God instructed him to leave behind – all. Specifically, Abram, as we will see, needs to get rid of a Lot!

Abram arrived in the land of Canaan and then on toward the hill country east of Bethel and pitched his tent with Bethel on the west and Ai on the east. About this time, a famine which was very severe struck the land of Canaan and this forced Abram to journey down to Egypt to live there as a foreigner. There were some very interesting events which happened in Egypt which we will discuss in a later chapter. When Abram left Egypt, he was escorted with much added wealth in addition to what he already had. Abram had become rich in livestock, silver, and gold and he journeyed back to the hill country of Bethel where he had pitched his tent before.

We know that Lot still accompanied Abram and he had also accumulated flocks, herds, family, and servants. The land where Abram settled could not support both the livestock of Abram and Lot, so there were arguments which broke out between Abram's herdsmen and Lot's herdsmen. There were two other groups living in the land as well, the Canaanites and Perizzites. So, four groups were vying for resources from the land to support themselves and their animals.

Abram, wisely, came up with a solution to the problem. Because he did not want to quarrel with Lot, he told Lot to choose which portion of the land he wanted to settle. Abram told Lot that if he chose the right, Abram would settle on the left. If Lot chose the left, Abram would inhabit the right. He gave Lot the choice of the land before him.

"Lot lifted his eyes and carefully surveyed the land around him all the way to Zoar". (Genesis 13:10 TPT) We have seen Abram lift up his eyes before and discussed this at length in his encounters with God. Lifting up one's eyes is significant especially if they are focused on the target God has placed the center of everything else. Abram lifted his eyes to get a vision of just how many descendants he would have by looking into the night sky and seeing the countless number of stars. Abraham (as he was later called) looked up on his journey with Isaac to the land of Moriah and saw the mountain where the sacrifice would take place.

Here we see Lot lifting his eyes and the vision before him is nothing but mere carnality. He can only see in the natural what is plainly before him. He has no concept of the promise of God. He chooses what appears to be the best and suits his own interests. He excitedly tells Abram that he will take the Jordan Valley. It is fertile and reminds him of where they had just come from, Egypt. The place where Lot settled was in the lowlands near Sodom, where the people "were extremely wicked and rebelled against Yahweh" (Genesis 13:13 TPT).

Lot is now living in close proximity to a place just like God told Abram to leave behind. Lot is comfortable settling near wicked people, idolaters, occultists, just like there were in Ur. Lot and his family are rubbing elbows and intermixing with the culture of Sodom. They are not separate. They have both feet in Sodom.

Abram did not, himself, choose the land before giving Lot the first choice. Abram knew that even if he were to have the least desirable portion of land, God would provide. The blessing of God had been with Abram and in his journey, he miraculously acquired even more wealth, even in Egypt. Because of Lot's affiliation with Abram, he had also flourished. Lot had protection with Abram and there was covering for him and his family. The anointing was on Abram and therefore, flowed to those who accompanied him. Lot was foolish to think he could separate from Abram and do well on his own without help from Yahweh.

The name Lot means "covert," "secret," or "concealed".[32] The old wicked ways were still hidden or concealed in Lot's heart. This is why it was so easy and natural for him to choose the portion of land near the wickedness of Sodom. Lot compromised and he was lured away from the blessing. Wickedness tugged on his fleshly heart and he consented. Lot, even though physically hundreds of miles from Ur, had never really left. What was pleasurable to his eyes and comfortable to his heart and what he tried to protect out of self-interest would be burned up in the flames in the judgment of Sodom and Gomorrah.[33]

So, Lot separated from Abram and took the well-watered and fertile Jordan Valley near Sodom and Abram settled in the land of Canaan. This separation would not have been necessary if Abram had left Lot at the start of his journey. Here, the natural result was not enough resources for both men's people and animals. The quarreling and strive could have been eliminated if Lot had remained in Haran.

Although we aren't entirely sure why Abram allowed Lot to come on the journey with him, I can only hypothesize. Abram's deceased brother, Haran, was Lot's father. Perhaps Abram tried to be a father figure to Lot in the absence of Haran. Perhaps Abram just had a soft spot for Lot and was trying to help. Whatever the justification, the separation between Abram and Lot needed to happen for Abram to be in full obedience to God's instruction of leaving all, including Lot.

Even though Lot was nearby, the separation had officially occurred. It was at this point after Lot separated from Abram that God encountered Abram the third time. It was only after separating that God could give Abram more revelation. It was in this encounter that God told Abram to lift his eyes and in any possible direction he could see, the land would be for him and his descendants forever. He told Abram to get up and walk through the land, to put his feet on it. By doing this, Abram would be taking dominion over the land and bringing it into his own possession.

We just discussed that Lot lifted up his eyes. No doubt, Lot was surveying the same land that God now told Abram to behold. The difference is that God instructed Abram to do this and it is God-centered, not Lot-centered. Abram had selflessly not chosen the choicest portion of land, but in giving Lot the choice, he scooped it up. Abram had not only separated from someone who was not supposed to be on his journey, but had also proven himself to be selfless, trusting in the provision of God.

Even though Lot had separated from Abram, this is not the last we will see of Abram's nephew. Unfortunately, Abram will still have to deal with his Lot which will include a military mission to rescue him from some kings who have taken him captive.

What we find next is the first war mentioned in the Bible. Even though, to us today, it seems very localized, it was then an international war.[34] There were four kings who had conquered several city-states. The four kings who were the victors were Elamite, Amorite, Harrian, and Hittite. They mandated that the five city-states pay tribute to them. The five city-states did this for twelve years and had had enough, so they stopped in year thirteen. The following year, in year fourteen, the four Mesopotamian kings gathered their armies and together went to let these five city-states know who the boss was. Their aim was to severely punish and in the military exploit, they, as victors, took many prisoners and completely sacked the cities. One of these cities was Sodom. One of the prisoners of war was Abram's nephew Lot.

Lot and his family and all his possessions were carried off by the punishing war lords. There was one, who escaped this wrath, and came to tell Abram that Lot had been captured and carted away with the other prisoners and loot. Just when Abram has made the separation with Lot, he enters the story again in an urgent and tragic way.

Abram has settled by the oaks of Mamre the Amorite. Mamre had two brothers, Eschol and Aner. They were allied with Abram by a treaty. Abram had made friends and had an alliance of those sworn to protect each other and help in times such as this. Abram did not hesitate or debate about what to do. After he heard what happened to Lot, he mobilized all the men in his camp. He prepared them and organized his rescue effort. Abram was now drawn into this international conflict and was about to lead 318 men to take on and defeat the four warrior kings.

Lot had not been taken by one man or even one family. Lot was captured by four kings with their own armies which had united with passion because of greed and pride. They wanted to maintain their status as the ones in power and to continue receiving the wealth from the lowly city-states as tribute payment.

If Lot had been a prisoner of one or just a few, it would have been easy for Abram to defeat these aggressors and it would have been a matter of duty and honor to rescue his blood relative. However, that is not the case here. Lot is in the hands of who knows how many men who had blood lust and domination pumping in their veins. Between the four kings, their armies could have numbered in the thousands of men. However, Abram had 318 men. These men had been born and trained in his own household.

Abram had not just been out gazing at the stars and daydreaming. He had not just been passively overseeing the livestock, seeing the newborn increasing and multiplying his herd. Abram was prepared in the case of warfare on himself or his family. For the 318 men who would be Abram's army, it says they had been trained. Abram knew the risk and challenge that was a potential threat to himself and his family and possessions. He did not rely on others to protect him, even though we know he had allies in the region. Abram had been actively training those born in his household to defend and protect, as well as serve offensively. It is clear that Abram had become wealthy with the amount of servants he had born in his household. These servants were trained men and they did not leave following Abram by just picking up a spear or sling to crudely try and defeat the enemy. One of their functions, in addition to everyday duties, was to provide and serve militarily. They were very capable of making a successful attack.

We find that Abram and his men pursued the invaders as far north as Dan. Abram was very wise in his military strategy. He attacked during the night and divided his forces to defeat the enemy. When Abram's men attacked, they recovered all the stolen possessions, but they brought back Lot with all the women and the other prisoners. Abram did not only liberate Lot, but he freed all the other prisoners including women.

How could Abram be so successful with a force that seems so small compared to the more massive size of the enemy? Obviously, God was with Abram. God had promised Abram seed and descendants too numerous to count. I believe that Abram had faith that he would make it through this battle and return to see his promised son. God's blessing was upon Abram. Even though he was few in number, he was powerful and had a supernatural military strategy. His decision to attack at night and divide his men into different battalions attacking from different positions proved successful. In addition, there was time and effort spent in training these men before the conflict arose. Lastly, I believe that Abram was motivated by more than what these prideful and greedy kings wanted. The love Abram had for his nephew and the bond he felt with Lot was so powerful, Abram's military rescue was immediate, with wise strategy, and well executed. It was lean and mean.

Abram did not have to enter an international conflict. He was not part of it. The conflict was between four kings to five city-states. Abram could have remained an isolationist. He could have just reasoned that Lot had chosen to live in a place of wickedness instead of remaining and honoring his uncle. Abram could have been resentful that in the face of all Abram had done for Lot, he chose what looked better and separated from Abram. Instead, Abram was a family man, which is probably why he allowed Lot to come on the journey from the beginning. Abram had most likely stepped in as the father figure to Lot after the death of his own father, Abram's brother. Abram may have even seen Lot as the child he did not have yet, his own promised son.

For whatever reason, it is clear that Abram acted without hesitation, and he used his own men and own resources to fund this rescue effort. He knew it would take time to travel and pursue these invading kings and eventually rescue Lot. Yet, he did it anyway. I don't believe he thought about acting any other way. I believe that Abram was so bound by duty and honor that he would have gone even if it was alone.

Abram's men were thorough. They did not just rescue Lot and then leave. They acted thoroughly and completely, bringing back all the other prisoners and women as well as all the possessions that the enemy kings had carried off. Abram led a mission which recovered all.

Even though Abram has now acted with duty, the highest honor, and is now completely victorious, it was a serious distraction to what otherwise would have been normal life. He had to take 318 strong men from his place of settlement, and they could not take care of their normal duties back home for some time. Abram had to risk his life as well as the lives of his men. In addition, Abram funded the military mission himself. He spent part of his own wealth to make it all happen. So, he has spent rather than saved. If Lot had not come on his journey, if Abram had specifically indicated that Lot could not accompany him from Haran, this involvement in international conflict would not have had to occur. Abram would have been spared from lost time, energy, wealth, and perhaps unknown number of his own men who died in the battle.

In addition, those who stayed home and did not go on the military mission were most likely taking on roles of those who had gone to fight. There would have been an extra burden surely on those left behind to keep things running smoothly as well as keeping those people and possessions protected. Entry into this war was a sacrifice that is seen on multiple levels. Lot's presence, even nearby, is distracting and causing everyday life to be uprooted.

Even though Lot should not have been on the journey from the beginning, he nevertheless was, and his nearby presence is not the best that God has for Abram. However, God is so good and full of mercy. He is with Abram, even in dealing with the consequences of his partial obedience. Abram is growing in character and maturity. We see that when he returns from the war, he does not keep any of the spoils for himself when given the opportunity. He also, is quick to give a tithe, or a tenth, of his assets to Melchizedek (which we discussed in lengthy detail in Part 1). Abram is a giver, not a taker, a man of integrity, duty, and honor. He puts God first by tithing and not taking spoils that go to the king of Sodom. Abram wants to let the world know that God has given him wealth rather than ever allowing someone to believe his wealth was acquired from the unrighteous spoils belonging to Sodom.

Lot has now been rescued. He and his family and all his possessions are now back where they were before they were captured. Well over a decade later, after Abram left Haran, Lot has established himself in Sodom. He initially pitched his tent toward Sodom, now he has a permanent dwelling inside the city. He is still nearby and Abraham (his name has been changed) has settled near the oak grove of Mamre. Abraham has a powerful encounter with three men, one of whom is Yahweh. In the last part of this encounter, Abraham walks with Yahweh and the other two toward Sodom. God shares with Abraham that He has a task ahead which is to visit the city and see if the wickedness and corruption is as severe as the cries for justice coming from the people there. God must judge the city.

Abraham knows that the judgment could and would most likely be destruction of the city because with wickedness was so severe. Abraham must have turned his thoughts toward his nephew, Lot. Again, Lot comes to the front and center of what we see next as bold intercession from Abraham for the righteous people of Sodom. Abraham asks God if he will spare the city for the sake of 50 righteous that could be found there. God answers that he will indeed spare the city for 50 righteous. Abraham then asks the same question but for the sake of 40 righteous people. God consents to spare the people for the sake of 40 righteous people. Then Abraham asks for 30, then 20, and finally ends with 10 righteous people. Still, Yahweh tells Abraham that he will spare the city for the sake of even 10 righteous people.

Ten is the number of people Lot has in his family. There was Lot, his wife, his daughters and their future husbands. Abraham has ended his intercessory pleas knowing that this is the number of Lot's family. Abraham has once before physically mounted up and gone to rescue Lot through military expedition. Now, he is once more rescuing Lot, but through intercession, or spiritual warfare.

As we find out, the two angels do go on to the city of Sodom and strongly persuade Lot and his family to leave the city because it will be destroyed. The perversity in the city is rising high and even the people try to sexually molest the angels (they appear as men). The angels even grabbed the hands of Lot's wife and daughters and brought them outside the city because Yahweh was so merciful. When the angels are finally able to get Lot and his family out of the city, the instructions are clear. The angels tell them to "Run for your lives! Don't stop anywhere in the plain until you've reached the mountains. And don't even look back, or you'll die" (Genesis

19:17 TPT)!

By mid-morning, Lot arrived at the small village called Zoar and then God proceeded to send His fire from heaven to annihilate the cities of Sodom and Gomorrah. Everything, including the people, and all in the city was completely eradicated.

"But, Lot's wife turned and gazed longingly on the city and turned into a pillar of salt." (Genesis 19:26 TPT) Here we see the evidence of what was in the heart of Lot's wife. Even with very explicit instructions to not look back knowing the result would be death, Lot's wife turned and gazed longingly on the city. She turned. She was headed in a forward direction but turned completely backward in her vision. She did not have her eyes on what was ahead, but on what was behind. This is even more telling in that she gazed longingly at Sodom. A gaze is more than just a look, it is looking and taking in the site and savoring the sight. Her heart was aligned with Sodom. Her heart agreed with the culture and lawlessness and evil that was rampant in Sodom. And she was Lot's wife. Because they were married, they were unified. They were one in body, soul, and spirit. Even though Lot did not physically look back, his "other half" did. A wife reflects an enormous amount of her husband for the world to see.

As we saw in the choice Lot made when he had any part of the land to choose from, he chose what was pleasurable to the eye, the fertile valley near this place of wickedness. It wasn't just Lot's preference. Lot's wife was in agreement.

Yahweh did honor Abraham and remembered his love for Abraham when he spared Lot and his family, ultimately destroying Sodom and everything within her boundaries.

That morning as Abraham hurried to the place where he had spoken face to face with Yahweh, to intercede for Lot and looked over plain to where the bustling cities of Sodom and Gomorrah had just been.

He saw the billowing smoke from the fire of God that had thrashed every last shred of evil from its existence.

Lot began with his uncle Abram, who had been called by God and had been promised by this same God great and wonderful things. The blessing was oozing all over Abram. Lot, in his journey with Abram, had prospered because he was under the covering of Abraham. Lot received the protection of Abram, twice! Once through physical warfare and the second time because of spiritual warfare intercession. We see that it was because God remembered his affection for Abraham that he spared Lot from all the destruction of Sodom. (Genesis 19:29 TPT)

The lesson is clear as to why God told Abram to "leave it all behind" including his native land, his people, and his father's household (most especially his nephew, Lot). There is such a sad ending to Lot's story. Lot was afraid to remain in Zoar, where he had fled to escape the burning destruction of Sodom. We learn that he ended up settling in the hill country and lived in a cave with his two daughters. He goes from abundance, blessing, and protection to lastly fathering children by his daughters. The daughters are afraid that they won't be able to have children and so they come up with a scheme to get Lot drunk and each become impregnated by him. This is what they had to do to preserve their family blood line. Lot's family, through his influence had sunk this low.

I believe that it is very clear that Lot should never have been allowed to begin the journey with Abram. Obeying God in every small detail of his instructions is important and critical. Even though God has shown up in powerful and merciful ways, much pain and sorrow and loss could have been avoided if Lot had been told to stay in Haran. Even though so much could have been spared, Abraham has seen God work in his life, has seen faithfulness time and time again, and has through all the mistakes, learned and has grown. God does work everything for our good and He certainly does this in

Abraham's life. "So we are convinced that in every detail of our lives is continually woven together to fit into God's perfect plan of bringing good into our lives, for we are his lovers who have been called to fulfill his designed purpose." (Romans 8:28 TPT)

In leaving it all behind, we are to leave old mindsets, old habits, and old influences. Romans 12:2 (KJV) says, "Do not be conformed to this world, but be transformed by the renewing of your mind, that you may prove what is the good and acceptable and perfect will of God." Another translation says this very beautifully, "Stop imitating the ideals and opinions of the culture around you but be inwardly transformed by the Holy Spirit through a total reformation of how you think. This will empower you to discern God's will as you live a beautiful life, satisfying and perfect in his eyes" (Romans 12:2 TPT).

By leaving it all behind, Abraham is finally able to leave old mindsets, cultural norms, expected participation in certain events, and even influence of family members. God wants Abraham to be completely renewed and transformed. Yahweh wants Abraham's mind and heart and wants him to be committed to all His ways. Abraham can only receive the magnitude of the promise when he has pruned his life in this way creating mature growth.

"You will keep in perfect *and* constant peace *the one* whose mind is steadfast [that is, committed and focused on You—in both inclination and character], Because he trusts *and* takes refuge in You [with hope and confident expectation]." Isaiah 26:3 AMP

CHAPTER 5

She is my sister: Abraham and then Isaac

We consider and honor Abraham today because of his mighty exploits of faith, sometimes seemingly as if he were a fictional character or a superhero. It is easy to sensationalize the strength of one's legacy and allow it to grow to be larger than life. However, in order to learn from Abraham, we must remember that he was human, just like you and me. Abraham had to go through the process just like we do. Abraham did not start out as a great faith hero. He began as the son of an idol maker.

Just as there are good days and days with challenges, we soon find that even though Abram was walking with promise and was living in the land that was flourishing with milk and honey, a severe drought struck the land of Canaan. Abram's faith is about to be tested.

The Egypt Experience as Half-Siblings

Not only did Abram experience a severe famine in the land, but Isaac, and Jacob did as well. Of course, Joseph, through his trials, really had been set up to rescue his father, brothers, and the entire family. Faith will always be tested, and for the patriarchs, this is especially true. I believe that there is special significance that the promised land, the one promised with abundance which is to sustain and be the inheritance for Abram and his uncountable descendants, would be struck with severe famine. Abram has been promised that this land is his and for his successive generations of children.

However, before him is a land whose soil is seemingly devoid of the ability to bring forth life.

Abram had journeyed from a life filled with idolatry, wickedness, and any form of a twisted way of life because God called him and gave him instructions to go to the land that God would show him. This land is God's promise to Abram. Abram didn't just get in his car and drive for a few hours and then arrive in the greatest of comfort. He didn't hop on a plane and take a nap and wake up at the destination. He traveled through rough ground with his herd and animals, his wife, and servants for days and weeks. We aren't told how long it took Abram to travel from Haran to the land of Canaan, but it took a while. It was dusty and dirty. Their feet were covered daily in the dust and soil of the ground. They had to stop and set up camp to rest and then pack everything back up to continue the journey. A man, whose father and ancestors, did not know God, heard the voice of God and obeyed. But obeying was not just for Abram to say "Yes" and then it was over. The "Yes" required uprooting his life and travelling miles and miles and miles to this land of Canaan with the hope that Abram really did hear from a God with a great promise. There must have been times when Abram questioned himself, especially early in this journey and early in his faith walk.

One of those times was early after his entry into the land of Canaan. A severe and devastating famine struck the land of Canaan which forced Abram to travel down to Egypt to live there as a foreigner. Abram had been living in the hill country of Bethel with Bethel on his west and Ai on his east. From there, Abram had journeyed the entire length of the land from north to south. He had covered the entire territory in stages and had journeyed through the southern desert, the Negev, as well. He was not that far from Egypt. The famine is so devastating that Abram could not stay and survive in the land of Canaan. There wasn't just a drought or a slight shortage of crops or water. This was so extreme that Abram had to physically leave the location to survive.

Even though we know that all the people who were with Abram, including Lot and his family as well as the servants, traveled with him and left Canaan, the passage in Genesis 12:10-20 only refers to Abram and Sarai leaving and traveling to Egypt. However, I believe this is for emphasis regarding what happened in Egypt. We do, however, know specifically that Lot travelled to Egypt with Abram because in Genesis 13:1, it refers to Lot returning to Canaan from Egypt with Abram. Abram would have taken all his possessions and all the people with him to avoid starvation. In Egypt they could all survive the famine.

So, Abram and Sarai entered Egypt and had to live there as foreigners. What we will see in this experience in Egypt as well as two more similar experiences (one with Abraham and one with Isaac) is that living as a foreigner exposed Abram (or the person living as a foreigner) in ways that they were unexposed to living in their own land.

If a woman was desirable or attractive or was just someone that another man wanted, they would take her by force in some cases. The laws were very different in those days and their customs were not like ours today. As Abram neared Egypt, we see the humanity of Abram rise up and emotions of fear and anxiety give voice to what is in his heart. "When he drew near to Egypt, he said to his wife Sarai, 'Look, *I'm worried* because I know that you are a beautiful, gorgeous woman. When the Egyptian men take one look at you, they will say, 'She is his wife.' Then they will kill me in order to have you. Just tell them you are my sister so that they will treat me well for your sake and spare my life" (Genesis 12:11-13 TPT).

This is an example of seeing the process of faith work in someone's life. Abram, did not start out in his juvenile faith years as "The

Father of our Faith". He was a man, born in the flesh, just as you and me. He had weaknesses, but he also had a heart that wanted to be postured toward God. This is a key. Even in the growth process and even in falling short, God knows exactly what is in our heart, our intentions, and the composite of our innermost being, and He sees us for exactly who we are and more importantly, who He has created us to be. "For the word of God is living and active *and* full of power [making it operative, energizing, and effective]. It is sharper than any two-edged sword, penetrating as far as the division of the soul and spirit [the completeness of a person], and of both joints and marrow [the deepest parts of our nature], exposing *and* judging the very thoughts and intentions of the heart." (Hebrews 4:12 AMP)

It is clear here what was the intention in Abram's heart. He wanted to save himself. He was afraid that when the men in Egypt saw how beautiful his wife was that they would kill him to have Sarai. Abram is already dealing with survival issues having fled Canaan to literally survive. He has now packed up camp, a massive endeavor, and loaded all his possessions and all the people with him and he is once again, traveling to a place he has never been before. Even though his journey may be at a walk's pace, his mind is running wild with every bad and terrible "what if" scenario that could happen in Egypt.

Isn't this so typical? You receive a promise from God and you say "Yes, I want that promise and I receive that promise!" Then you start on the journey and you get a little into the process and encounter a hurdle. You have a little success, but not quite enough to combat the fear that shows up screaming in your face about everything that is about to go wrong. Abram was in the exact same position. He was probably tired from the journey. We know that he communicated this plan to Sarai as they were nearing Egypt, so they were almost at the end of the days of walking through the heat and sand. Abram's mind most likely was also heavy from weighing the options of what to do – stay in Canaan, leave Canaan, pack everything, leave a little behind to lighten the load, will they kill me to have my wife, etc. The mind is a battleground, sometimes even more of a key battlefield than the physical ones. It is in this mental battleground where the outcome is determined.

"For who has known the mind and purposes of the Lord, so as to instruct Him? But we have the mind of Christ [to be guided by His thoughts and purposes]." (I Corinthians 2:16 AMP) It is very important for us to have, not our mind, but exchange it with the mind of Christ. This verse is a promise, and if we take it, it says that we have (we already have it) the mind of Christ. But we must renew or make it new daily.

Romans 12:2 (AMP) says, "And do not be conformed to this world [any longer with its superficial values and customs], but be transformed *and* progressively changed [as you mature spiritually] by the renewing of your mind [focusing on godly values and ethical attitudes], so that you may prove [for yourselves] what the will of God is, that which is good and acceptable and perfect [in His plan and purpose for you]." I really like this translation of the verse. It emphasizes in detail exactly the process you must go through to renew your mind. It is what we see happen in Abram's life and it is what will happen in our own lives if we apply its instructions.

We have discussed in detail the initial instruction God gave to Abram which was to "leave it all behind" (Genesis 12:1 TPT). God does not want us to be changed to fit the mold of the world around us. Sometimes, that means leaving the world around us and moving to a different environment. We need new values and customs. This was very evident in the values and customs of Ur and Haran where wickedness was celebrated. In order to change the mind and have the mind of Christ, we must be transformed or formed in a way that becomes according to and modeling or being the mind of

Christ. A key here is that this is a progressive change. This is something that is continually happening. It doesn't happen all at once. It is part of a maturing process, just as a baby grows and gets stronger and moves from just milk to solid food. The baby grows, but the eye can't detect growth as it is happening. But soon enough, all the sweet little baby clothes are too small for the big baby. Then, before you can blink, the baby is taking his first steps. There are some markers along the way that are visual, but growth happens at a slow, but hopefully consistent pace.

The same is true for renewing the mind. You can't always tell when it's happening, but if it is consistent, then you can see change occur. Focusing on godly values and ethical attributes as a lifestyle promotes mind renewal. We should be patient and full of mercy to those around us and with ourselves, understanding that renewing of the mind is something that is a process. This is not to say that because it is a process, we have a license for acting outside of the ways of God, but that we should be ever hungry and vigorously striving to grow in how we think like Christ. It would be very easy to criticize Abram at this point and say that he fell short, which is factually true, but in order to learn and grow and see how this man grew in his relationship with Yahweh (and do the same in our lives), we must see how his faith walk increased and he eventually became so rock solid that he is now known as "The Father of our Faith"!

Traveling to and living as a foreigner in another land lead to vulnerabilities. The Hebrew root *gwr* means "to tarry as a sojourner" and could possibly have been derived from words that mean "to attack, strive" and "to be afraid"[35]. In the culture of that day, a person would have family or other alliances or relationships in place for protection. There are examples of gangs of men seeking to rape other men and women sojourners in the Bible (Genesis 19:1-11 and Judges 19). In order to be protected, you would need a group of men whether it be family, trained servants, and alliances for safety and well-being. Traveling to a foreign land opens the vulnerability and means potentially less protection. This is why Abram was traveling with his family and servants (as well as their families). The idea is that larger number of sojourners traveling together, the greater the ability to protect each other. However, entering into foreign land presents problems of submitting to the rule of the king or ruler there and hoping for the best.

In order to survive famine and outrun death, Abram must go to Egypt and survive death there, albeit from other situations. He fears the men will kill him to get him out of the way in order to have his beautiful wife. It is out of fear that Abram tells Sarai to tell the people in Egypt that she is his sister. Abram knows that if the people there believe that Sarai is just his sister, this would offer them more protection than if they believe she is his wife.

Sarai was Abram's wife, obviously. However, she was also his half-sister. Sarai and Abram had the same father, but different mothers. By saying that Sarai is his sister, is factually true. However, their primary relationship is husband and wife, not half-siblings. We find Abram implying that he is not married to Sarai by telling the truth. He used the truth to imply something that was untrue.

The questions for our purposes are: Did Abram act in faith? Did he need to tell everything? Did he need to give all the facts? Is it ok for him to just tell the truth just enough even though it implies something untrue?

We know that Jesus never fell short and that he never once sinned. Even though he was fully God, he was fully man at the same time. His life on earth is meant to show how we can and should live, being fully human ourselves. There is an interesting story in John chapter 7. Jesus did not give his half-brothers all the information but held back some information. They wanted Jesus to go to Jerusalem for the Feast of Tabernacles, to proclaim to the people who he was.

But Jesus said that he was not going yet because his time had not yet come. He stayed in Galilee and when his brothers had gone, he went secretly.

Here, we see that Jesus did not give his brothers all the information. They did not know he was going to go to Jerusalem in secret. He traveled on a backroad and went without making himself known. Jesus did this because he was acting in accordance with His Father's timeline. His brothers were not entitled to this information that was not given. Jesus was acting in obedience and in faith. His heart posture was toward the will and full obedience to God.

The answer to the questions is to look at the heart posture. It is certainly wise and prudent to not reveal certain information to people. Not everyone is deserving or entitled to every piece of information. Jesus did not lie. Abram did not lie. However, there is a difference between the heart posture of Jesus and of Abram's. Abram's words convey his heart posture. He said these words to Sarai, "I'm worried". (Genesis 12:11 TPT) Abram was afraid. He was not acting out of obedience to an instruction of God. Unfortunately, he wasn't acting from a posture of faith here.

By calling Sarai his sister instead of his wife would mean that a negotiation would have to occur with Abram, her brother, before the men in Egypt could have any interaction with her. If Abram was thought of as her husband, the men could just kill Abram to get him out of the way. This is definitely a troubling moral dilemma, but ultimately decided from the posture of the heart – a posture of faith or one of fear. Abram believed that if he just told this version of the truth that the chances of both their survival would be good.

Just as Abram feared, the men saw Sarai's stunning beauty when they arrived in Egypt and praised her to the Pharaoh. She was taken into the Pharaoh's palace and made part of his harem. Sarai was at least 65 years old, yet she was stunningly beautiful.

Because of Sarai, Abram's life in Egypt seemed to be very smooth and he got along well. He received royal treatment from the Pharaoh who gave him "sheep, cattle, male and female donkeys, camels, and male and female slaves" (Genesis 12:16 TPT). Abram is growing in tremendous wealth during his stay in Egypt. Instead of being killed as Sarai's husband, Abram is rewarded as Sarai's brother with great wealth.

We truly see the blessing of the Lord evident in Abram's life. God's promise to Abram is His word. Even in the shortcomings of Abram, in allowing fear to be his voice, Abram is living in blessing in a foreign land. In a land where Abram feared death, Abram is abounding in wealth. Not only did Abram survive famine to escape to Egypt, we see that God's hand of protection and blessing is on him – in spite of his shortcomings. God is working everything out for Abram's good (Romans 8:28). Even though Abram has acted out of fear, I believe the innermost part of Abram's being is indeed drawing toward God and God has seen his heart. God has also made a promise to Abram, which we know will surely come to pass.

God has promised Abram seed and Sarai is his wife. Even though God has not specifically promised that Sarai would be the mother of this promised child (God later specifically promises this), Abram is now in a predicament where his wife-sister is now part of Pharaoh's harem. We don't know if the marriage by Pharaoh to Sarai was ever consummated, but I am venturing out to say that I do not believe so. What happens next is that Pharaoh and his household are stuck with terrible diseases because he had taken Abram's wife.

Somehow Pharaoh knew that the reason for the disease that had come upon him and his household was because of Sarai being taken into his harem. This could have been from a dream or a vision. We know that in another similar event which we will discuss next, that

King Abimelech had a dream alerting him that Sarah was Abraham's wife. (Their names had been changed by that point.) However, Pharaoh did know and was not pleased.

Abram had kept information, vital information, that Pharaoh believed he was entitled to have to avoid a catastrophe. Because Pharaoh lacked this important information and did know that Abram was in fact Sarai's husband, there was something even greater at risk other than the disease that struck Pharaoh and his household. There was the potential that the promise son for Abram would be thwarted because his mother is now the wife of Pharaoh. In addition to putting Pharaoh into a position of violating his own cultural standards of having another man's wife as his own, the plan of God and the bigger picture now has clear evidence of tampering. However, in God's goodness, he is able to reign back the situation and his guiding hand is apparent by his protection of Abram and Sarai.

I believe that God was protecting Abram and Sarai by the allowance of disease to plague Pharaoh and his household. It was an attention getter for Pharaoh that something was terribly wrong. The conclusion, obviously, that Pharaoh had was that the cause of this horrible thing was due to his possession of another man's wife in his harem. The only remedy was to immediately make Abram and Sarai leave. Pharaoh gave orders for his men to escort Abram and Sarai out of Egypt along with everything he had, including all his immense wealth he had gained there in his role as Sarai's brother.

By acting in fear and telling the Egyptians that Sarai was his sister, Abram potentially endangered Sarai by failing to protect her as his wife. By telling a "righteous lie" or "a little white lie," Abram was not protecting the one he is supposed to protect – his wife. Abram was acting to protect himself. He was afraid of death, which is why he left Egypt and schemed to only portray their relationship as siblings. Abram will learn in his journey the relationship of the bridegroom to the bride. When someone doesn't have a specific revelation, it proves challenging to live it out to its fullest. The ultimate example of this relationship is with Jesus and his bride – the church. To be intimate with Jesus and to know the extent of his love for us is to know safety and protection as well as love. Jesus didn't try to save his own life at the expense of making his bride vulnerable. He went in the opposite extreme. Jesus gave his live to protect his bride (John 3:16).

The Gerar Experience as Half-Sibliings

Twenty-five years later, Abraham and Sarah (their names are now changed) arrive in another foreign land as siblings again! They have been living near the oaks of Mamre and now have traveled to the southern region of Canaan to live temporarily as a resident of Gerar. Gerar was a very wealthy place and was a Philistine city-kingdom in the south of Gaza. The king there was named Abimelech.

We see a repeat of what happened twenty-five years earlier in Egypt. Abraham is living in a foreign land without same protections he would have in his own land. We do know that over the years, Abraham did increase in wealth greatly and he is now a very wealthy and powerful man. Abraham has hundreds and hundreds of servants as well as animals. We are not sure why Abraham and Sarah have gone to Gerar to settle, but we know that their intention is to be there temporarily.

Abraham told the people in Gerar that Sarah was his sister. Because she was his sister, the king of Gerar, Abimelech, sent for Sarah and took her or abducted her into his harem. At this point, Sarah was about ninety years old. It is interesting that a king, with the choice selection of women, would want a ninety-year-old woman and desire her to be in his harem. Just as she was at age sixty-five in Egypt, Sarah, was still stunningly beautiful and God had supernaturally rejuvenated her youth and made her attractive, even to a king. According to Jewish tradition, "her flesh was rejuvenated, her wrinkles smoothed out, and her original beauty was restored".[36] The Dead Sea scrolls likewise comment on Sarah's miraculous restoration due to her faith in the promise of God with these words: "fair indeed are her eyes…and all the radiance of her face…and her hands now perfect. Her legs how beautiful and without blemish her thighs… And when the king heard the words of [his three officials], he desired her exceedingly, and he sent [them] at once to bring her to him, and he looked upon her and marveled at all her loveliness…and he (God) sought to slay me".[37] I believe that Sarah's youth was supercharged supernaturally. Psalm 103:5 AMP says this about God: "Who satisfies your years with good things, So that your youth is renewed like the [soaring] eagle". God really did prove his word by the dynamic and supernatural rejuvenation of Sarah.

Once again, Sarah is in the hands of a king who is not necessarily an ally of Abraham. He could prove to be a deadly enemy. Once again, the king has taken Sarah because of her stunning beauty. And once again, it is because the king believes Sarah is only Abraham's sister.

God appeared to Abimelech in a dream one night and told him, "You're as good as dead, for you have taken into your harem a married woman" (Genesis 20:3 TPT)! We discussed in great detail Abraham's encounters with God in Part 1. We see that God encountered the Abimelech, the pagan king, the enemy king to keep him from sinning and touching Sarah. Abimelech recognized that God was visiting him in this dream and heeded the stern instructions. It was a wake-up call for sure!

Even though Abimelech took Sarah with a clear conscience, believing that Sarah was the sister of Abraham and certainly not his wife, Abimelech still had the potential threat of death as a consequence of even his "pure" action. In addition to being threatened with death, Abimelech's entire household was cursed and became barren, not being able to conceive or bear children.

In the dream, God told Abimelech to return Sarah because she is Abraham's wife and that Abraham would pray and intercede for Abimelech and his household because he was a prophet.

Abimelech rose early the next morning and immediately called for Abraham. He told him that God had visited him in a dream and that now because of Abraham's lack of telling the full truth, there are serious consequence at hand. Abimelech must obey and return Sarah and now they are under judgment and curse. Abimelech asked Abraham why he did this and acted in this way. Abraham's answer is very telling. "Because I thought, 'There's no one here that fears God. They will kill me to get to my wife.' Besides, she really is my half-sister. She's my father's daughter, but not my mother's, so I married her. When God sent me out to wander from my father's house, I said to her, 'Here is how you can show your love for me. Everywhere we go, you must say about me, 'He's my brother.'" (Genesis 20:11-13 TPT)

Just as we saw the heart posture of Abram in Egypt, here we see once again that fear has crept up and we see a repeat of what we saw in Egypt. Abraham is afraid that the men in Gerar will want Sarah because she is so extremely beautiful and they will kill Abraham because he is her husband. If Abraham is thought to be her brother, his life may be spared.

Just as Pharaoh was severely displeased because of the disease that came upon him and his household, here Abimelech is outraged because Abraham has allowed Abimelech to put himself into a position to bring forth curse and death on himself and all his household. Abimelech is put out and gives Abraham his wife back, just as God had instructed to spare his life.

Here, something slightly different occurs. Whereas in Egypt, Abram was given wealth in the form of animals and servants because he was Sarai's brother, here we see that Abimelech gives Abraham sheep, cattle, and both male and female servants after the sibling scheme and consequences are discovered. In addition, Abimelech told Abraham that his land is before Abraham and that Abraham can settle wherever he pleases.

In addition, what in a way seems like mockery, Abimelech tells Sarah, "I am giving your *brother* a thousand pieces of silver as compensation to settle any claim against me, to exonerate you in the eyes of all who are with you, and to clear your reputation" (Genesis 20:16 TPT, italics mine). Just to emphasize that this is all because Abraham is Sarah's brother and this is the way Abraham allowed their relationship to be known, Abimelech gives additional wealth in the form of silver as compensation for any negative harm that was done. This is kind of like punitive damages that Abraham received. The initial sheep, cattle, and servants are given as actual damages, but the additional thousand pieces of silver are given for the pain and suffering, and potential bad name Sarah may have received as a result of being the wife of two men.

So Abraham's fear of death is not realized, but again he has been covered in the mercy and grace of God. When Abraham does not tell the full truth to save his own life because of the fear of death, he walks out of the situation unscathed and wealthier than ever. He also has the choice of the land before him from the word of the king - in a foreign land.

Something that I personally find interesting is that Abraham was afraid of death. His fear could have been anything. It could have been a fear of lack, a fear of disease, a fear of other people, or even a fear of spiders, but we see repeatedly a fear of death. Abraham had a fear of death, but the promise of God to him was a promise of life. This is why these two separate events which are so similar – the first one in Egypt and the second in Gerar – are specifically written in the Bible. We are to learn from these. Our faith is to be built and we are to be inspired. Our hope is to be encouraged. Abraham, The Father of our Faith, was afraid of death, but God promised him life. When his body was as good as dead and Sarah's was well past childbearing age, God kept his promise to Abraham to bring forth seed from him and multiply it to numbers that we can't even count. Abraham, we will see through his journey of faith, had to trade faith in fear for faith in God. In faith in God, the promise of life comes.

As we discussed in great length in Chapter 2 of this book, Abraham did pray for Abimelech and his household. We know that Abimelech's life was spared and because of the great intercession from Abraham for Abimelech and his household, the curse of barrenness was broken, and the women began to conceive and have children again. Their legacy was preserved because of the prayers of Abraham. Go back and revisit that chapter. Abraham, the prophet, while still waiting on his own promised son, his seed to be harvested, and his descendants to become as numerous as the stars of the sky, prayed for the very thing he was waiting on himself for someone else. He prayed for the wombs of the women in the household of Abimelech to be opened. And God heard his prayer and answered.

The situation in Gerar could have been devastating. It could have resulted in the premature death of Abraham and even Sarah. It could have resulted in a lot of hypothetical bad situations. However, God turned it around and used it for Abraham's good and for his benefit. He increased tremendously in wealth. He and Sarah were both protected physically, and their reputations were restored. Abraham's ability to intercede for others flourished. We see this even actually propel Abraham into the realization of his promise being manifested. After Abraham prayed for the wombs of the women in Gerar to be opened and their infertility was healed, we see the very next paragraph in the Bible (although it goes into a new chapter) that

"Yahweh visited Sarah, just as he said he would, and fulfilled his promise to her. And Sarah conceived and bore Abraham a son in his old age, at the exact time God had promised them. Abraham named his son Isaac, the miracle son, whom Sarah bore him" (Genesis 21:1-3 TPT).

Even though Abraham fell short, God never falls short. Even though Abraham was afraid. God is a God of faith. "If we are faithless, He remains faithful [true to His word and His righteous character]..." (2 Timothy 2:13 AMP)

Gerar, the Sequel with Isaac and Rebekah

Like father, like son.

Isaac, the son of promise, is now an adult and his is married to his very beautiful wife, Rebekah. Just as in his father's day, there is a famine in the land. When Abraham experienced the severe famine, he was forced to flee to Egypt. However, God told Isaac not to go down to Egypt, but to stay in the land God would reveal to him. Isaac traveled to Gerar where Abimelech was the king. This could have been the same Abimelech as was the king during his father's stay there.

We see here something distinguishing up front. God has given Isaac instructions about where to go and where to stay during this famine. Just as Abraham had many encounters with Yahweh, we see here that this is one of many encounters Isaac has with Yahweh. "Live there as a foreigner, and my presence will be with you. I promise to bless you, for I will give all these lands to you and your descendants. I will fulfill the oath I swore to your father Abraham. I will make your descendants as numerous as the stars of heaven, and I will one day give them all these lands. I will bless all the nations of the earth through your offspring because Abraham was faithful to me. He listened to my voice and yielded his heart to follow my direction.

He kept my commandments, my instructions, and my teachings." (Genesis 26:3-5 TPT)

God has promised to bless Isaac during the time of famine in a foreign land. We saw that Abraham was also blessed during a famine as well in Egypt. We aren't sure of the reason Abraham journeyed to Gerar, but it is also evident that Abraham prospered there as well. God confirms the promise he made to Abraham to Isaac.

Isaac must have grown up hearing about God's faithfulness firsthand from his father and from his mother. Isaac surely had heard the stories and the encounters that his parents had and their journey for over twenty-five years of waiting on Isaac to be born, when in the natural everything looked hopeless. Isaac has been filled to the brim with faith-filled stories from his father, "The Father of our Faith" himself.

Isaac isn't just starting out on his own journey from nowhere. He has some shoulders to stand on. These are not just any shoulders, they are of Abraham, the man, the Patriarch himself. Abraham really started on his faith walk from the very beginning. His father was an idol maker from Ur, the place of utter wickedness. He started from nothing - no knowledge, no parenting in the form of godly training, nothing. But God took him to a place of rock-solid faith.

Isaac is much more fortunate. It would provoke one to jealousy to realize the starting vantage point Isaac had in terms of knowing, understanding, and living out faith in a relationship with Yahweh.

Isaac obeyed the Lord and settled in Gerar. Just as if we had pressed the rewind button, we see Isaac (just as we saw twice with Abraham) was filled with fear that he might be killed to clear the way for the foreign men to approach his wife, Rebekah. The men did find Rebekah stunningly attractive. But Isaac was afraid to tell them she was his wife. Just as his mother, Sarah, was supernaturally rejuvenated at age 65 and even age 90, Isaac's wife was also breathtakingly beautiful.

After Isaac had lived in Gerar for a while, the king, Abimelech, saw Isaac through his window caressing his wife Rebekah. Abimelech knew at that moment that Rebekah was Isaac's wife, not his sister. Abimelech summoned Isaac and questioned him about his relationship with Rebekah asking why he did not tell them the truth. Isaac tries to explain, "Because I thought the men of the land would kill me and take her" (Genesis 26:9 TPT). Isaac reveals here his true motivation for telling the lie. He was afraid of death, just like his father had been.

Rebekah was not Isaac's sister. She was his 2nd cousin. Rebekah's grandfather was Nahor. Nahor and Abraham were brothers. Isaac does in fact tell a lie about his relationship with Rebekah. Whereas Sarah was actually Abraham's half-sister, Rebekah is Isaac's 2nd cousin. Abraham told the truth, just not all the truth. Isaac here tells a lie.

Abimelech is furious. He tells Isaac that one of the men may have violated Rebekah and then brought guilt and punishment upon the people. Isaac has put the men and women of Gerar in a precarious position. Abimelech then orders the people of Gerar to not put a hand on either Isaac or Rebekah or they will suffer the punishment of death.

Here, just as in both instances with Abraham, Isaac is now living with protection for his life and Rebekah's according to the order of the king of Gerar. He has entered the land with the fear of death permeating his thoughts. Now, his life is protected.

Isaac is the promised son. He has been brought forth against all odds in the natural as a promise of life. His life was promised by God long before he was even conceived. The promise saturated Abraham and continues through the life of Isaac for the realization of descendants. At this point, Isaac and Rebekah have no children. Yet, Isaac has been born and is a living testament to the promise of God. He just needs to see his own reflection to see the faithfulness of God. Yet, he is smitten with fear of death. However, in spite of Isaac's shortcomings, the promise of God to him and also for the sake of Abraham's faithfulness will stand the test of time and adversity.

Just as God promised Isaac when he entered Gerar, God fulfilled his promise and has rescued his life and Rebekah's life. God also made his harvest there bountiful. Isaac planted crops in Gerar and in the same year while the famine was ravishing Canaan, reaped a hundred-fold harvest. Yahweh blessed Isaac greatly. In the land of Gerar, Isaac became extremely wealthy and grew in riches, acquiring flocks, herds, and servants. In fact, he became so prosperous that the Philistines became extremely jealous of Isaac. They tried to stop up his wells which were the same wells that Abraham had dug. This was an act of war on the part of the Philistines because water was a lifeline. To stop up someone's well was an extremely aggressive act.

Isaac reopened the wells of his father Abraham and went on to dig and open his own wells. The well signifies the source of life, the source of water for our existence. Abraham dug some of these wells which represent his faith walk, his learning and drawing from the well of Yahweh. Abraham made progress by leaps and bounds in his journey, but was a man who had shortcomings. He learned. He persevered. He got back up and kept going and eventually, through consistent walking with the Lord, growing in faith, received the promise. Isaac, drew from his father's wells, standing on his shoulders, drawing from his lessons of faith. Isaac could not just draw from the same wells that Abraham dug. Isaac had to dig his own wells also and encounter Yahweh for himself. Even though Abraham is the great Patriarch, "The Father of our Faith," Isaac could not only ride on his father's coattails. He needed his own suit designed by the Creator and was fitted specifically for him.

Instead of fighting back against those who waged war against him, Isaac just moved on to a new area. Isaac is building character and growing in his own faith, just like Abraham built character and had to travel down his own faith journey. God allowed Abraham and Isaac, through their tests to fall short, but learn in the process.

Eventually, Isaac became so wealthy in the land of Gerar and Abimelech became so jealous that he told Isaac to leave because he had become too rich and too powerful. So Isaac left the jurisdiction of Abimelech and camped and settled near the Wadi of Gerar. God's promise of complete protection and blessings are evident in Isaac's life. God's presence was with him. And God continued to bless Isaac. Again we see, "If we are faithless, He remains faithful [true to His word and His righteous character]..." (2 Timothy 2:13 AMP).

CHAPTER 6

The Ishmael Before The Isaac

One of the very first passages we read in Genesis about Abram after we learn his family genealogy is when God encounters him in Genesis 12. This is the first time we know of when God spoke to Abram and clearly laid out instructions and promises for Abram. The promises revolve around two primary blessings: a promised land that God will show Abram and Abram will be made into a great nation with uncountable descendants. This chapter is meant to focus on the second part, Abram being made into a great nation and specifically his promised son (which God will further clarify in later encounters to Abram).

The journey of faith Abram traveled to believe God that this promise could be true as well as the unfolding and timing of actually receiving the promise is so completely inspiring and at the same time so relatable. We admire Abram and his faith accomplishments. In order to learn from the Patriarch, we must acknowledge his journey. We must reconcile the fact that he wasn't perfect from the beginning and there were shortcomings along the way. But, the beauty of his journey is that he didn't stop short, even in the face of failures. He kept going. The comforting and reassuring part is that God never gave up on Abram. He never went back on his word or broke his everlasting covenant with Abram. God stayed true even when Abram fell short. God was the stabilizing factor and the supernatural component that ensured Abram's success.

We know that when God spoke this promise to Abram that he would be made into a great nation that he was about 75 years old.

Abram was married to Sarai who was about ten years younger, so she was about 65 years old. For their entire married life, Sarai had been unable to conceive children. She was barren. At the point when this promise was spoken by God to Abram, it was a far stretch in the natural for this to be realistic. How could Sarai, who was 65 years old, conceive a child? She had been barren her entire life. Now, not only was she barren, but she was a couple of decades past being able to conceive children. Even if she had been very fertile in her younger days, she was already well past the age of being able to conceive.

What an outrageous promise. Today, when a woman is pregnant and the birth will be when she is 35 or over, she is treated differently by her physician. She is looked at as having a higher risk for many conditions and there are more tests recommended than if she were younger. I remember going for a visit when I was pregnant, and the baby was due when I was

35. I was very young and healthy, and I felt like my physician treated me as if I were geriatric. I did not like being treated that way at all, especially since I was 34. Imagine the feeling of being Abram and Sarai at ages 65 and 75, receiving such a promise that seemed so unlikely from God.

Ten years go by. There is a decade of more of the same kind of humiliating barrenness. Day after day, week after week, months pass and now ten years have come and gone. Sarai isn't getting younger. She is now ten years older than she was when Yahweh spoke this promise of descendants to Abram. So many events have happened in this ten-year period.

Abram has been forced to escape to Egypt to survive the life-threatening famine in Canaan. He told the Egyptians that Sarai was his sister because he was afraid that he would be killed so that the Egyptian men would be able to have Sarai, seeing how beautiful she was. Pharaoh was outraged because he took Sarai into his harem and because of this, Pharaoh and his household were struck with horrible diseases. Pharaoh had his men escort Abram out of Egypt with great wealth which was given to him by Pharaoh.

Abram and Lot eventually separated because the land could not support both of their livestock and people. Lot went to live near Sodom in the Jordan valley and Abram settled in the land of Canaan. Abram later enters into an international conflict and takes his fighting men to go rescue Lot because he has been taken a prisoner of war by some enemy kings. Abram is successful in battle and rescues Lot and all his people and possessions and brings them home safely. Abram gives a tithe of all his assets to Melchizedek after the victory.

In the middle of all these dramatic events, God continues to encounter Abram and speak to him, further confirming His promises to Abram. God gives Abram instructions to follow and in the midst of war and peace, conflict and resolution, there is growth in Abram which is evident in the eyes of Yahweh. Abram is not perfect, but Abram has a heart for God. Sarai is with Abram through all these events, trials, and victories. Yet, Sarai is still without a child.

Sarai is now 75 years old and Abram is 85. Sarai is the same age that Abram was when he received the promise of descendants from God. I think that Sarai's age of 75 is worthy of emphasizing for that reason. She knows that when Abram was 75, the spoken word from Yahweh came to Abram with a promise of descendants. Sarai was Abram's wife. Wouldn't it be logical that Sarai would be the mother of the promised child? Yet, ten years later, Sarai is still not a mother.

So, at 75 years old, Sarai comes up with a strategy. Abram receives the promise from God at age 75. Now, we find Sarai, at age 75, has brainstormed a solution for the problem. Genesis 16: 1-2 TPT says, "Now Sarai had borne no children for Abram. She had an Egyptian slave girl named Hagar, so Sarai said to Abram, 'Please listen. Since Yahweh has kept me childless, go sleep with my maidservant. Perhaps through her I can build you a family.' Abram listened and did what Sarai asked."

This passage is so telling. Sarai had for ten more years seen nothing come from this promise of God. She was now even older and still not a mother. So, she had a plan. Who knows how long she had thought of this plan, but the fact remains and that is she had solidified the strategy and now thought it was the right time to tell Abram. Hagar was the solution. Hagar was Sarai's maidservant, her Egyptian slave girl. There is a tradition that says Hagar was the daughter of Pharaoh. When Abram was expelled from Egypt, Pharaoh had given Abram wealth and servants. It would make sense that Sarai would have a servant from all that Pharaoh had given.

It was not uncommon for a maidservant to be called upon if the primary wife could not have children. The maidservant would become a secondary wife to the master and through her, there would be a legacy of children. This was Sarai's strategy. Sarai was convinced that since all she had experienced was barrenness, the only way for Abram to have children would be through her maidservant. Since Hagar was Sarai's property, the child or children through Hagar would be credited to Sarai. The words Sarai used clearly reveal the condition of her heart on the matter. She says in speaking of Hagar, "Perhaps through her I can build you a family" (Genesis 16:2 TPT). The word "perhaps" is hopeful, but not completely confident. The meaning here is that even with this Plan B, this scheme of Sarai's heart, she wasn't entirely sure if there would be a son for Abram. Beyond this, the more telling part are the words "I can build." Sarai was trying to make this promise come about. She must have had a type A personality with a plan B in her heart. She wanted to make this happen. She was tired of not seeing any movement on this. She wanted Abram to have a son and she wanted to make sure this happened.

Sarai was trying to build the family instead of letting Yahweh do it. This plan was Sarai's plan and not God's plan. There is a word play in Hebrew. The words for build (*baneh*) and son (*ben*) are very similar[38]. Sarai wanted to build the promise son herself. She wanted to take over the direction of this project because she was tired of waiting. It appeared that nothing would ever happen for her, and this would hopefully ensure that Abram would have a son.

"Abram listened and did what Sarai asked." (Genesis 16:2 TPT) Abram listened to his wife and it seems, passively did what she asked. He did not argue with her or encourage her to just be patient. He did not go to God and ask if this was the course of action to follow. He just listened to Sarai and did what she asked. Maybe he knew that arguing with Sarai or bringing a different perspective would not go over so well with her. Maybe Abram was tired himself and this seemed like a good idea. Whatever the rationale, Abram agreed by his actions and he consented with this Plan B by aligning himself with the strategy.

So Abram took Hagar to be his second wife and she conceived. The plan is working. Hagar is now pregnant. What should be joy is almost immediately squashed because Sarai's plan is now working against her. When Hagar realized that she was pregnant, she began to belittle Sarai and make fun of her. Sarai told Abram that it was totally his fault that Hagar despises her and he needs to stand up for her. Sarai even said that Yahweh would judge who was right.

Sarai had a fleshly plan, a plan B to produce or build Abram a son. Now, Sarai is not only building a son for Abram, but a mess, and the mess is not in her favor. God's plan for us is good and is a blessing, never bringing a curse with it. His plan is the Plan A. "The blessing of the Lord brings [true] riches, And He adds no sorrow to it [for it comes as a blessing from God]." (Proverbs 10:22 AMP)

Abram's response to Sarai seems to be still in the passive category. He doesn't say, "Sarai, it was your idea for Hagar to be my second wife. You created this situation because you wanted Hagar to get pregnant and have a son for me. Can you just be considerate? Hagar is pregnant now. Just let her be." This wasn't the response from Abram. Instead, he put the responsibility on Sarai and didn't want to be responsible for the repercussions of the discipline of Hagar. Abram told Sarai that Hagar was her slave girl and under her authority, so do with Hagar whatever she wanted. I think that Abram was trying to keep Sarai happy and appease her instead of truly do what was right in the entire situation. His actions appear to be passive instead of taking a stand for what was right.

So, Sarai mistreated Hagar and because of the cruelty, Hagar ran away into the wilderness. Hagar was pregnant and upset. The angel of Yahweh visited her and instructed her to go back and to humbly submit other mistress, Sarai. The angel told her that she would give birth to a son and that she was to name him "Ishmael." This name means "God hears" or "May God hear". It also signifies being born of the flesh.

The angel told Hagar characteristics of Ishmael. He would be wild and difficult to tame. He would be hostile to everyone and he would live at odds with his kinsmen. These characteristics of Ishmael are not only evident in his life but began to show themselves through Hagar even upon his conception. There was animosity between Hagar and Sarai and there was hostility and from this time until Abram ultimately sends Hagar and Ishmael away, they lived at odds with Sarai (and eventually Isaac). This prophecy of character shows up in history as well, even to today, in the hostility, animosity, and difficulty of the descendants of Ishmael living in a world with the descendants of Isaac. We see this in the enflamed conflict in the Middle East that is so prevalent.

Something beautiful happens as a result of this encounter with the angel of Yahweh. As Hagar is in the wilderness, having fled because she was suffering from mistreatment, feeling anguish, and knowing that she is pregnant with Ishmael, the Lord hears her cries of distress. Even the name the angel instructs Hagar to name her son is evident that the Lord has heard her cries and that God hears her. Hagar called God a special name after this encounter, "You are the God of My Seeing" (Genesis 16:13 TPT). It is beautiful to know that God saw Hagar in her valley. Even though Hagar had not been perfect (she had made fun of Sarai), God still saw Hagar and heard her cries. Hagar was one of the main characters living and fulfilling the scheme of Sarai's Plan B. Hagar was the backup. She wasn't the one Abram loved. She was used and taken to fulfill a plan for someone else. She felt abused and neglected. But God saw her and in the face of her despicable situation, He encountered her. God made a promise to her. Her promise was different than the promise He made to Abram. But God kept His promise to each of them despite their own humanity and shortcomings.

After the encounter with the angel of Yahweh, Hagar returned, and Ishmael was born. Abram was 86 years old when Ishmael was born. This is 11 years after God encountered Abram with the promise of a son. Now, Ishmael is born. The only problem is that Ishmael is not the son of the promise. He is a son of the flesh.

When Abram was 99 years old, Yahweh encountered him, and his name was changed to Abraham. Yahweh also changed Sarai's name to Sarah during this encounter. Also, Yahweh outlined his covenant with Abraham and gave him instructions that would serve as a sign of Abraham's part of the covenant being upheld. Abraham was to take off of the males in his household, born in his household even as a servant or purchased, and circumcise them on the 8th day of their birth. For all the men already well past 8 days old, Abraham circumcised them that very same day. So, Abraham and Isaac were both circumcised that day. This sign of circumcision was to show that flesh had been cut off. It was symbolic of cutting away of physical and fleshly desires and instead having desires and promises birthed through the leading of Yahweh.

Abraham was circumcised when he was 99 and Ishmael was 13. Ishmael was not conceived through his father being circumcised because Abram (as his name was then) was not circumcised when Hagar conceived Ishmael. Ishmael was conceived through flesh. However, we will see that the promised son, Isaac, is conceived through circumcision because "Yahweh visited Sarah, just as he said he would, and fulfilled his promise to her. And Sarah conceived and bore Abraham a son in his old age, at the exact time God had promised them. Abraham named his son Isaac, the *miracle* son, whom Sarah bore him. When Isaac was eight days old, Abraham circumcised him, as God had commanded him" (Genesis 21:1-4 TPT).

"Isaac" can mean "laughter," but a more complete and full meaning would be laughter in the past tense or "delayed laughter." After conceiving and having a child at 90 years old, Sarah laughed, and this laughter was full of joy and the realization that God did fulfill his promise. God fulfilled the promise of delayed laughter on his own. God did not need anyone's help to bring this about, most especially Sarah's. God alone fulfilled his end of the bargain, his promise, his Plan A, his Isaac.

Twenty-five years after God gave Abraham the promise of a son, Isaac is born through his wife, Sarah. At the time they received the promise, Abraham was 100 years old and Sarah was 90. This is God's plan for Abraham, his original promise that never changed, his plan A. God kept his promise to Abraham. "So, it is impossible for God to lie for we know that his promise and his vow will never change!" (Hebrews 6:18 TPT)

After Isaac had been born and he had been weaned, there was a great feast to celebrate his transition from baby to older child. During the celebration, Sarah noticed that Ishmael was mocking Isaac. Just as Sarah reacted when she was belittled by Hagar, again, Sarah told Abraham to get rid of Hagar and Ishmael. Sarah did not want Ishmael to be a co-heir with her son Isaac. This was the breaking point with Sarah. She tasted her own soup concoction, and it wasn't good. She needed a new recipe. She needed Hagar and Ishmael banished. Sarah's plan B turned out to backfire and she just couldn't stand by and watch it escalate anymore. Sarah was fiercely protective of Isaac.

Just as before, Abraham listened to Sarah's wishes. However, this time (we have discussed this in a previous chapter) God spoke to Abraham after he heard Sarah's wishes. God told Abraham to not be distressed over Sarah's wishes, but to do whatever Sarah asked concerning Hagar and Ishmael. God confirmed to Abraham that it would be through Isaac that the promise of descendants would come. However, to ease Abraham's mind and comfort him due to his love for his son Ishmael, God also assured him that Ishmael would become a great nation as well, but the promise would rest on Isaac.

Abraham obeyed the Lord and early the next morning, he gathered some few provisions for Hagar and Ishmael and sent them away into the wilderness of Beersheba. An angel of God protected Hagar and Ishmael in the desert and Ishmael grew up in the wilderness of Paran. The scripture says that he became an expert archer.

Both Ishmael and Isaac's names are descriptions of what they brought to their mothers. Hagar had fled from the mistreatment of Sarai and was alone, pregnant, and crying out in desperation in the desert. The angel of Yahweh instructed Hagar to name her son "Ishmael" which means "God hears" or "May God hear." This is a picture of misery crying out in a lonely forsaken place, but God hears us in those places.

Sarah had waited for twenty-five years since the promise of God to her husband. She had been subjected to humiliation that resulted from barrenness. In her culture, it was a very shameful thing if a woman could not conceive. She had been painted with a negative mark on her. While women around her enjoyed the birth of their little ones, she was left to just watch. Even when she took matters into her own hands and had Hagar step in her place to conceive Ishmael, she had to just stand by with no natural children of her own. She had not been able to participate in one of the greatest joys of life, one that she had waited so long for and one she never thought would really happen for her. When Abraham had an encounter with Yahweh, he was instructed to name his soon coming son

Isaac. "Isaac" means "delayed laughter." How fitting for Sarah to be 90 years old and have her own biological child, a son, for Abraham, fulfilling God's promise and bringing so much delayed laughter!

The names of the mothers of these two sons are also very descriptive and tell us more about Ishmael and Isaac. Hagar was Sarai's maidservant. She was from Egypt, and probably became Sarai's maidservant during the time that Abram and Sarai had fled Canaan for Egypt to escape a terrible famine. There is a Jewish tradition (we discussed this earlier) that tells us that Hagar was the daughter of the Egyptian Pharaoh, who gave her to Abram after he had seen many miracles that followed Abram and Sarai. The name "Hagar" can mean "ensnaring" or "stranger." In Aramaic, it could mean "fugitive."[39] The plan B came through a stranger to the promise, one who acted like a snare to trip and stumble and forfeit the promise. Even though God did protect Hagar and kept a promise for her, with respect to the promise God have Abram, by the meaning of Hagar's name we find that this was not the plan A for achieving the promise of Isaac. Instead of delayed laughter, there was a crying out in distress.

Hagar was from Egypt and perhaps was Pharaoh's daughter. In the Bible, Egypt is symbolic of the world, of things unspiritual or material. Egypt is a picture of slavery and bondage. The mindset of Egypt is that of a kingdom ruled by philosophy and the natural and physical senses. It opposes God. Egypt, in so many ways, is like the place where God took Abram from Ur of the Chaldees. This place was a place of demonic fire and flames. God wanted Abram to leave this all behind, this place, these people, these relatives, this way of life, the wickedness, the lawlessness, the idols, the bondage - the low life. The plan God had for Abram was to take him from this kind of world, this kind of kingdom and transition him to a new land, a new kingdom, and have going from him a new nation of people.

"Sarai" and "Sarah" (as she was later called), both mean "princess." There is really no difference in the meaning of the old version of her name versus the new version of her name. However, during the encounter when Yahweh changed Abram's name to Abraham, Yahweh also changed Sarai's name to Sarah. Both Sarai and Abram needed new names so they could see new identities for themselves. They each needed something new, something fresh, and something in the newness of a name to launch them into the next step of receiving the promise. Even though Abraham's new name had more significance in the change of meaning, Sarah still received a new name and with this she would be able to identify with her transformation to actually be the mother of Isaac.

There is a lesson from these two sons, Ishmael and Isaac, that we learn from Paul in Galatians 4. Paul tells the Galatians that there are two kinds of covenants and two women symbolize these two covenants. There is Hagar and Sarah. The first covenant birthed its children into slavery as represented by children born to Hagar. Hagar represents the law which was given at Mount Sinai by Moses (after Abraham). This correlates to the earthly Jerusalem of today and those people who are living in bondage.

"In contrast, there is a heavenly Jerusalem above us, which is our true 'mother.' She is the free woman, birthing children into freedom!" (Galatians 4:26 TPT) Paul says that "we're now the true children who inherit the kingdom promises" (Galatians 4:28 TPT). These are royal proclamations for our benefit, describing in detail our inheritance as true sons and daughters. We are not children of the slave woman; we are children of the free woman. We are sons and daughters of Grace.

Ishmael did not inherit anything from his father's estate. He was expelled with his slave mother into the wilderness to be separated forever from Abraham's kingdom and estate. Isaac received a full inheritance of all his father's estate as the sole beneficiary, not sharing with any other takers including Ishmael. Before Abraham died, one of his last acts for his son was to ensure that the right and proper wife had been secured for Isaac. Abraham had his trusted servant, Eliezer, swear that he will choose a wife for Isaac among the relatives in his native land, not from among the Canaanites. The story is beautiful in that Eliezer traveled to Abraham's native land and prayed specifically regarding some character traits that

would stand out in the woman chosen for Isaac. The fulfillment of this prayer and is that Rebekah is chosen to be Isaac's wife and when Isaac sees her, he falls in love with her. Abraham, in one of his final acts, has secured the right wife for Isaac, something like a father's blessing in a bride, which will be crucial in shaping the dynamics and the next generation of his legacy. Rebekah is chosen according to the wishes of Abraham for his son Isaac.

Ishmael married also, but Hagar arranged a marriage for him with an Egyptian woman. Just as we looked at the symbolism of Egypt with Hagar in how that fits in with the promise of God, here we see Ishmael's mother as Egyptian, but his wife as well. Ishmael is connected with the world in his conception, and he will perpetuate this worldly nature through his union with his wife to the next generation. Whereas Isaac is the sole heir of Abraham, Ishmael is disinherited. Whereas Abraham's blessing covers the select choice of a bride for Isaac through oath and prayer, Hagar arranges a marriage for Ishmael staying in the way of the world with an Egyptian woman.

"The law requires, grace empowers," is something I have typed into my "notes/to-do" list that I read every day. I have read this every day for several years. Something about this really speaks to me, maybe because in my daily work life as an attorney, I am digging in the trenches of the law. There is a beauty in the law, but there is also bondage. The law is supposed to create a framework of safety for its followers, boundaries of protection for those whose arms it protects. The law is supposed to harbor and protect and be a refuge for those who obey and against those who disobey. The problem is that following the law is impossible to do completely. No one can keep every part of the law. There are too many laws to even be aware of them all. Even in the practice of law, I understand a certain area (and am continually learning) but leave other areas of law to colleagues who understand those respective areas. It is impossible to keep and follow every law and every commandment (as in the law of Moses). This becomes a chore. It is hard work and the very thing that started out being for good becomes the enemy. Legalism, or working rigidly to follow the law, becomes the focus instead of the One who put the boundaries in place for our protection. The law requires. But Grace is far better than law. Because it is impossible to keep the law, Grace steps in and does what the law could not do. Grace is a person. Jesus is His name. Jesus empowers us and through our love relationship with Him, we possess the drive to passionately follow Jesus. Out of our zealous and spilling over love for Jesus, we can't help but to do what all the laws in the world can't do – Love the Lord with ALL of ourselves and our neighbor as ourselves. This sums up all the laws and all the teachings and all the prophetic words that have ever been or will be.

This is the difference between law and Grace, requirements versus empowerments, bond versus free, circumcised versus uncircumcised, Ishmael versus Isaac, plan B versus plan A - work of the flesh versus the promise of God.

CHAPTER 7

Looking up – stars as a visionary picture (and sand on the seashore)

Habakkuk 2:2 (AMP) gives a profound key to follow when moving from where you are to where you are going. It says, "Then the Lord answered me and said, 'Write the vision and engrave it plainly on [clay] tablets So that the one who reads it will run'".

Anyone who has ever seriously endeavored to work toward a vision knows that you must write the vision and keep it before your eyes. I have heard it said often that you move toward your most dominant thoughts. Keeping the vision before your eyes, keeps it in sight and in mind. The reverse is true as well – out of sight, out of mind.

Business leaders create business plans to reach goals, to reach their visions. It takes a very skillful and talented team of strategists who understand what it takes to write the vision and make it plain before those who will travel down the path of achieving the vision. Creating the plan or the blueprint to achieving the vision is a science and an art form. If this groundwork isn't done well or with understanding of how the mind works to achieve the final vision, then there is a high likelihood that success will be forfeited in exchange for defeat.

A common technique used in laying the groundwork for achieving vision is the use of vision boards. So many successful individuals and business leaders use vision boards to keep an image of what they are projecting for the future before their eyes. The mind ultimately does not respond to written words as much as it responds to visual images. Therefore, having images of what you see in the future is critical to allowing your mind to embrace it as reality and not just a hoped-for dream.

Of course, since God is the master creator, He is the designer and author of this key principle to achieving dreams, creations of the imagination, and fulfillment of visions and promises. Romans 4:17 tells us that God called what wasn't in existence to become reality for Abram in reference to the promise of descendants. One major key for how God helped Abram in his journey to receiving his promised son was the use of vision.

One of the very first foundational principles regarding vision is that it must be God's vision and not merely their own. "For who has known the mind and purposes of the Lord, so as to instruct him? But we have the mind of Christ [to be guided by His thoughts and purposes]." (I Corinthians 2:16 AMP) When we have taken on the mind of Christ, then we are guided by His thoughts and purposes and the vision that He has for you will become the vision you have for you. The vision you had for yourself merges into His vision for you and in that oneness of vision is success.

Abram was set up by God from the beginning, but he still needed to follow the path of faith to achieving the vision. Abram didn't just contemplate about his future and start to act on his own thoughts about his life. He had a profound and life changing encounter from Yahweh. We know this encounter well and have discussed it in various aspects up until this point. "Now Yahweh said to Abram, 'Leave it *all behind* – your native land, your people, your father's household, and go to the land that I will show you. *Follow me*, and I will make you into a great nation. I will exceedingly bless and prosper you, and I will make you famous, so that you will be a *tremendous source* of blessing for others. I will bless all who bless you and curse all who curse you. And through you all the families of the earth will be blessed." (Genesis 12: 1-3 TPT) In this promise with instruction, God proclaims His vision and His promise for Abram's life. Abram receives the vision straight from the mouth of Yahweh.

A good definition of vision is what you see about where you are going, where you are headed, and where you see your destination. However, for our purposes and applied to our lives, we must add that it must align completely with God's vision for our lives. Then it is not just any vision, it is The Vision for our lives.

After God spoke the vision to Abram, he acted on it. He left Haran and traveled hundreds of miles over grueling terrain with his caravan of family and possessions. Abram began to move toward the vision God had given him. Abram relocated and eventually settled in the land of Canaan after he and Lot separated. In a previous chapter, we discussed Abram's relationship with Lot in detail as it relates to Abram receiving the promise of God. It is very clear that on the path to achieving Abram's vision, not everyone should have been on that same path. Specifically, Abram did need to lose his Lot and Lot should never have been allowed to depart Haran with Abram on this journey to vision.

In the very clear instructions that were initially given to Abram, God told him to "leave it all behind" (Genesis 12:1 TPT). To move forward toward vision, your eyes must turn forward and leave some things of the past in the past. God knew the critical importance of this, and this is why this was the first instruction He gave to Abram. In fact, God gave this instruction to Abram before He gave him the promise. God told Abram to leave it ALL behind. Abram's future was too big to hold on to the low life. Holding on to things of the low life results in no life or just a mere existence. Vision produces way more than existence. It ushers in life which produces more life.

After Abram separates from Lot, God uses the technique of

showing Abram the promise in a picture form, a visual for his eyes to see. Abram has come a long way from where he initially was, but he still has so much further to go to reach the fulfillment of God's vision for him. I believe that God knew that Abram needed some encouragement, some leading, and showing him a visual or image was the way to accomplish this. "After Lot separated from him, Yahweh spoke to Abram, 'Life up your eyes and look around you to the north, the south, the east, and the west. As far as you can see in every direction is the land that I will give to you forever – to you and your seed. I will multiply them until they are as numerous as the specks of dust on the earth. If anyone could count the dust of the earth, then our offspring could also be counted. Now, get up and walk through the land - it's length and its breadth. *All the land you walk upon* will be my gift to you!'" (Genesis 13:14-17 TPT)

What we see is that God gave Abram The Vision, but then used vision, here meaning images for him to see, to help Abram journey through the path to get to that destination. God told Abram to lift his eyes! Abram needed to stop looking down as opposed to where he needed to look which was to look up.

When Abram looked up, he saw land as far as he could see in every possible direction. What a vision of the expanse and the vastness of the land God promised him. Abram didn't just look north as far as he could see. He didn't just look south as far as he could see. He looked to the north and to the south and to the east and to the west as far as he could see. This is an image of expansion and increase. This is a lot of dirt and sand. God went on to speak over this vast area and told Abram that this is the land that He would give to Abram forever. There are no limits here. God has taken Abram from his past confinement and limitations to this new vision of unlimited provision and promise. What was in the past a product of the natural, the vision is the supernatural. Regarding Abram's offspring, God said they would not be able to be counted, just as vast as the specks of dust in the vision before him.

After seeing the unlimited potential in this vision, God tells Abram to get up and go walk on all this land. Everywhere Abram can put his feet is part of this promise. So, God has given Abram a visual to see, to take in with his natural senses, which will help usher in what is unnatural in the natural. Abram is at least 75 years old here and Sarai, his wife is at least 65. Sarai has been barren for her entire life, and they have no children. What is natural and seen is barrenness, lack, dried up, and with end. However, the vision or promise of God is supernatural and God gives Abram a natural vision to help his senses take in the wonderful promise he will eventually receive in the natural. The natural sees into the supernatural bringing it into the natural. This is the beauty of vision.

Vision helps align our natural body, soul, and spirit with the vision that already exists in the supernatural. When God spoke the promise to Abram, God had already fulfilled it, but Abram had to receive it and pull it into the natural realm.

God used this powerful technique of vision again in Genesis 15. Abram just had some interesting life experiences which was partly due to him allowing Lot to accompany him on the journey from Haran. It was clear that he should have left Lot behind in Haran as per the instructions of Yahweh which preceded the initial promise. However, Lot did accompany Abram. Even though they separated eventually and settled in different areas, Lot was still relatively close by. Abram had settled in Canaan and Lot had settled in the Jordan Valley with his dwelling so close to Sodom that he was living and daily rubbing elbows with the wickedness in the city.

Lot was captured by some kings that came to take prisoners and possessions and enforce their own decrees against Sodom and other cities. Abram found out from a messenger that Lot was taken captive and Abram went to rescue his nephew, Lot. Abram did not hesitate to enter this conflict and he left his settlement with his own men, resources, and went to take back his relative which had been taken. We examined this in detail in a previous chapter. The importance of this event is that Abram had just bravely and victoriously defeated kings in a David and Goliath kind of military action. Abram was seriously outnumbered in every way. Yet, God was with him and his group of military heroes and Lot benefited from this military victory. Abram brought Lot and his family and all his possessions back home.

Abram still has no children. He is still waiting on the promise. In the natural, life looks the same, but filled with hardships. Abram did not plan on entering a war, leaving home, taking his men, and risking all their lives to rescue Lot. Obviously, Abram loves Lot because Lot is his nephew. But I believe that Abram knows Lot's character well from the events that led up to their separation. Lot was selfish and only looked out for what was in his own best interest. Lot chose what looked like the best land to settle in and left Abram with what appeared to be less desirable. In so many ways, Lot is a burden to Abram and here, Abram is dutifully risking it all to rescue this nothing but trouble nephew.

Abram, most likely, needed encouragement at this point. Even though Abram was strong and exhibited valor in battle and saw victory, he still is waiting on something that he has not seen his entire adult married life – the promise of a son. God, in His goodness and all-knowingness, came to Abram in a vision.

Abram's main concern was that Eliezer, his servant, would be his heir because he had no son. Abram wants a son. He wants his natural heir to be he inheritor of all his wealth. Even though he trusts Eliezer (and even trusts him with finding a wife for Isaac later), Abram is painfully and passionately reminding Yahweh that He has not given him any children. In this encounter, God reminds Abram not to yield to fear. God tells Abram something beautiful which is that He is Abram's "Faithful Shield" and his "Abundant Reward" (Genesis 15:1 TPT).

Even though Abram has been victorious in battle, warring against enemy kings, and returning a hero, Yahweh will continue to serve as Abram's

"Faithful Shield." Yahweh is the one who protects Abram and in protecting Abram will protect his future. Yahweh will protect and guard the vision He has given Abram, which includes the promise of a son. God Himself will be Abram's "Abundant Reward" and only in God will the promise of a son be realized.

God gently corrects Abram, full of love, to tell him that Eliezer will not be Abram's heir. Abram will surely have a son from his own body! What happens next is visionary. God takes Abram outside his tent to look up again. Abram must leave his tent where there is a ceiling to his vision. There is an obstruction to seeing beyond a certain point. There is a barrier to the limitless sky beyond the confines of the tent. God tells Abram to "Gaze into the night sky. Go ahead and try to count the stars. He continued, 'Your seed will be as numerous as the stars!'" (Genesis 15:5 TPT)

God has Abram look at the ultimate vision board, the night sky with countless stars, to get an image of the magnitude of the blessing that is in store for Abram. What looks like no fruit after decades of marriage to Sarai is going to result in the most populous number of descendants. From one end of the night sky to the other. From what Abram can see in the sky to the galaxies beyond. This is the unending and limitless promise God has for the bountiful harvest of descendants for Abram. Abram need not look down or hang his head low. He needs to look up not only this night, but night after night and imagine each of those stars as his very own descendants.

I believe that this backdrop for God's vision board for Abram was chosen because of the endless and ever-expanding universe for Abram to visually see, but it was never going to be out of sight. During the day, Abram would know the night was coming and the stars would appear one by one, until the dark sky was lit with promise. Every night, night after night, Abram would be able to meditate on the vision and let it settle deep in his spirit until looking up was part of his identity and the source of his destiny. It would have been life changing to see this vision board once, but God arranged it so that Abram would be able to see it every night of his life. In the dark, when doubts come, when fear starts to rise up, all Abram would need to do is look up.

Similar to Abram, the psalmist in time of need and receiving vision for his life wrote, "I will lift up my eyes to the hills – From whence comes my help? My help comes from the Lord, Who made heaven and earth" (Psalm 121:1-2 NKJV). The power of looking up is important. The psalmist also says that "You lift my head when I bow low in shame" (Psalm 3:3 TPT).

Motivational speakers emphasize the importance of vision boards in achieving one's dreams. It is important to get a visual before your eyes so that your mind can get the image to see in that form rather than in word form. Just because you have an image and see it once, that is not enough. It is important to see it regularly and keep it before your eyes. Even in the secular world, the principle from scripture is being taught! God created an image for Abram – the night sky with all the countless stars – as a vision board for Abram to meditate on every night.

God didn't just use the sky and the heavens to give Abram vision. That vision is meant to prophetically provide an image of the coming attraction. God has used the sky and His creations in the heavens to provide a vision or a picture of his grand plan for all time as well. Isaiah 46:10 TPT tells us, "I declare from the beginning how it will end and foretell from the start what has not yet happened. I decree that my purpose will stand, and I will fulfill my every plan".

When God created the heavens and the earth, He already had a master plan of how eternity would unfold. He created the end and then started at the beginning. Every intricate detail and every larger-than-life part of creation works together for His plan and His glory. Even the story of redemption is written in the sky. We have a vision board that tells us the greatest story of all time.

David writes in Psalms 19:1-6 TPT: "God's splendor is a tale that is told; his testament is written in the stars. Space itself speaks his story every day through the marvels of the heavens, His truth is on tour in the starry vault of the sky, showing his skill in creation's craftsmanship. Each day gushes out its message to the next, night with night whispering its knowledge to all. Without a sound, without a word, without a voice being heard, Yet all the world can see its story. Everywhere its gospel is clearly read so all may know. What a heavenly home God has set for the sun, shining in the superdome of the sky! See how he leaves his celestial chamber each morning, radiant as a bridegroom ready for his wedding, like a day-breaking champion eager to run his course. He rises on one horizon, completing his circuit on the other, warming lives and lands with his heat."

God uses the heavens to be prophetically visual. If we get out of our houses as Abram got out of his tent, we can look up and see this amazing story, the gospel story in the heavens. God has designed man with a need to look up and be able to recognize and understand what He has written in the heavens including meanings of stars, signs, and constellations. Genesis 1:14 TPT tells us, "And God said: 'Let there be bright lights to shine in space to breathe the earth with their light. Let them serve as signs to separate the day from the night and signify the days, seasons, and years.'"

Every month, a new constellation rises in the sky allowing for all 12 constellations to be seen every year. Each year, the story told in the 12 successive constellations is told. It begins with Virgo the Virgin and ends with Leo, the Lion, which proclaims that the Lion of the tribe of Judah is coming back as John describes in the book of Revelation. Because God is the author of the Bible and because He is also the creator of the universe, the amazing story He tells is the same! God wants us to look up![40]

"Lift up your eyes to the sky and see for yourself. Who do you think created the cosmos? He lit every shining star and formed every glowing galaxy and stationed them all where they belong. He has numbered, counted, and given everyone a name. They shine because of God's incredible power and awesome might; not one fails to appear!" (Isaiah 40:26 TPT)

Here is a powerful summary from "Looking Up":

VIRGO: There is a Messiah coming. LIBRA: He will be a Redeemer.

SCORPIO: There will be a war and He will die. SAGITTARIUS: He will resurrect and conquer death. CAPRICORN: From His death, a living people will be born. AQUARIUS: He will pour out His Spirit upon them all.

PISCES: His people will multiply and bless the earth. ARIES: His Kingdom will come, and His will be done. TAURUS: He will return with His people on behalf of Israel. GEMINI: His people will be just like Him.

CANCER: He will never let go of the as His possession.

LEO: He will rule and reign supreme throughout the universe.

Abraham Lincoln so wisely said, "I can see how it might be possible for a man to look down upon the earth and be an atheist, but I cannot conceive how he could look up into the heavens and say there is no

God". How true Abraham Lincoln's statement is. God designed the heavens and the earth. He is the masterful creator. God has used the heavens as a billboard to show off. He has used the night sky to provide illustrations of His goodness. He has provided hope and a future by the unlimited canvas for vision. From the vision of the countless stars in the night sky to the redemption story, God is an advocate of vision. He, in fact, is the creator of vision. Vision was key for Abram to receive the promise. It is no different for you and me.

After Abraham's (as he was called later) promised son, Isaac, was born, you might think that Abraham could finally stop meditating on the promise. However, even after 25 years of waiting for Isaac, the birth of Isaac did not mean Abraham could move on from his consistency in faith or meditating on the vision. We know that when Isaac was a man (not a boy anymore), God tested Abraham and this is the famous story of the Akedah, or the Binding of Isaac. God commands Abraham to travel to a mountain He would show Abraham and there, he is to sacrifice Isaac to the Lord.

After 25 years of waiting and then enjoying the relationship with Isaac for probably 30 years into Isaac's manhood, Abraham has been having to carry out his part of the covenant with God. Part of this is faithfulness and being committed to the vision. However, here, God is asking Abraham to sacrifice the promise. How can Abraham sacrifice Isaac? He is the promise. He is who God promised to Abraham and he is Abraham's promise for more descendants. To sacrifice Isaac would be aborting the promise.

However, Abraham was obedient and faithful to God. He immediately set off with his servants and Isaac the very next day to Mount Moriah, the place where God would show him. Abraham is faithful during the entire journey there. He is ready to sacrifice Isaac. Abraham knows that God is faithful, even when he falls short. Through his journey, Abraham has learned lessons about creating his own strategy to help God out of a situation that seems hopeless. This would seem to be one of those situations, but Abraham remains faithful to the smallest detail. As Abraham raises the ax to plunge into Isaac, the angel of the Lord stops him and tells him not to lay a hand on Isaac.

Yahweh now knows the intensity of Abraham's faithfulness and his willingness to obey and trust even when it looks like it is not in his favor. As Abraham lowers the ax and lays it to the ground, he "looked up" and his eyes fell on a ram caught in the thicket. He took this ram and sacrificed it in Isaac's place to Yahweh. Abraham named this place Yahweh Appears. By looking up, Abraham saw the continued presence and provision of God. Abraham visually saw the ram after he looked up. It was this ram that was substituted for Isaac's life, sparing Isaac from death, and figuratively resurrecting Isaac from the dead.

God spoke to Abraham after he sacrificed the ram and said, "I solemnly promise you, by *the glory* of my own name, decrees Yahweh, 'because you have obeyed my voice and did not withhold from me your son – your beloved son, I will greatly bless you! I will make sure your seed becomes as numerous as the stars of heaven and as the sand of the seashore. Your offspring will take possession of the city gates of their enemies. Because you have obeyed me, the entire world will be blessed through your seed.'" (Genesis 22:16-18 TPT)

God confirms his promise to Abraham of descendants. In his words to Abraham here, God purposely again refers to Abraham's descendants being as numerous as the stars of heaven. Abraham has been looking at the stars for decades now since that encounter where Yahweh showed him the vision board for his future. Every night, Abraham has been able to meditate on the promise by looking at those stars that shined so beautifully prophetically being used as evidence that the promise would come to pass.

I believe God said something like this to Abraham: "I gave you The Vision. Then I gave you vision in the form of this imagery – the stars in the night sky – to keep you focused. This was for you to see night after night, which you have seen and kept before you. Now, you have been tested with your promised son, Isaac, and passed the test. I know your heart. I know the true nature of your heart, your love for me and your trust in me despite what my instructions to you may seem like. They seem contrary to my promise to you. But I will fulfill my promise to you. Because you have meditated on the vision I gave you of the stars in the night sky, here is another vision for you. Your descendants will be as numerous as the sand on the seashore. So, not only as you look up every night into the night sky, but every day also as you walk on the sandy earth, I have given you, know that no matter where you look, day or night, I have cast the vision before you. Your descendants will be so numerous, and I will surely bless you Abraham and fulfill my word to you."

One very famous verse is Proverbs 28:18 KJV which says, "Where there is no vision, the people perish". A few years ago, I read Dodie Osteen's book, "Healed of Cancer". Some do not realize the health crisis she walked through which literally aimed to take her life. She went from a picture of perfect health to frail, sickly, and weak. Cancer came to steal and kill her. Dodie knew God's promise of healing for her. She believed the word of God. But she did one thing more that made a profound impact on her healing process. While she could barely get through each day because the cancer was eating away at her health, she knew she had to get a different image in front of her. All she could see in the mirror was her failing body. She saw her weight loss and the effect of disease wreaking havoc on her physical body. She refused to look at this as an image of herself. Instead, she gathered pictures of herself when she was the picture of health and put them everywhere. She knew that she needed to see the vision of herself as healthy and completely whole.

Dodie Osteen did stand on the word of God for her healing. Today, decades later, she is the picture of health that she looked at when cancer tried to tell her otherwise. She kept the picture of what and who God said she was before her eyes. One of the interesting things I heard her say once was that the doctor who had given her the diagnosis (of death) died and she went to his funeral, not the other way around. All these years later, she is still sharing her wonderful healing testimony!

A movie that was released in 1997 called "As Good As It Gets" drives home the point which really gets to the heart of what most people struggle with at some point. Is this as good as it gets? Is this really how my life is going to be? I thought I would be further along than this by now. In the movie, Jack Nicholson plays a writer of romantic fiction named Melvin Udall. He is completely rude and obsessive-compulsive. He's sharp with everyone and lives a lonely, aggravated life until his neighbor asks him to watch his dog. He doesn't want to, but he is forced to help. His story is sad and lonely, and it is as good as it gets for him until a waitress, played by Helen Hunt, eventually and despite her frustration with him, begins to have some compassion for him which turns into a relationship.

I remember watching this movie a long time ago and thinking that Melvin's life was so pathetic. He really was the cause of his own problems. He pushed everyone away and so challenging to be around. Is this the kind of life to settle for? Sometimes, I think that people just look at where they are or how their life has been for so long and think that this is as good as it gets. This is the best it could be and there is no hope for the future.

This is not true and this is not biblical either. Joshua 1:8 and James 1:25 tells us to behold the Word of God. This is because what you behold or have visually in front of you, you will become. What you constantly look at you become. This is the law of vision.

The Bible also tells us that we are what we think in Proverbs 23:7. Abram did not have to settle for his old life, or even his life somewhere along the path to his promise. The intention and purpose of God was for Abram to cross paths with the promise, not travel the path to the promise and never get there. The destination is the promise.

Just as God used vision to help Abram achieve the promise, so God will give each of us vision as well to achieve promises he has for us. I encourage you to think of the promises that God has given you and write them down. Then get some visual images and pictures and put them on a vision board. Make sure this vision board isn't hidden or somewhere you never look. Just as God placed the night sky in front of Abram every night for him to see, you need to place your vision board in a place you will see daily. You need to consistently see the vision before you. As we discussed early in this chapter, your mind moves toward your most dominant thoughts. So, keeping the vision before your eyes causes your mind to meditate on those images. Just like Abram, look up and see the vision. Look to the future, not the past. Just like with Abram, there are unlimited stars in your night sky too.

CHAPTER 8

Abraham – Friend of God

In today's modern world, there has been confusion about the real meaning and definition of "friend." When you ask people what friend means, you may get a lot of different answers based on that person's background, social status, or their generation and age group.

In general, people may say that a friend is someone that you can spend time with, enjoy similar activities, talk to about more private matters, and someone you can trust. One of the first goals of traditional education is to make sure that children are socialized and learn how to interact with others. When a child is at home, under the wing of his or her mother, father, or other caregiver, that child is in a protected environment and typically the goal is nurturing of the child. At a certain age, usually when children are school age, they begin to socialize more and are placed in an environment with other same age children. These children become their friends.

In this environment, you may say that a friend is someone around the same age who is developing at about the same pace and learning similar things. Children who are the same age generally like to play the same kinds of games, watch the same kinds of cartoons, and think the same kinds of jokes are funny. If you mix an older child in with a younger child, you find that the dynamic changes. It is not so homogenous at this point. Either the older child will have to adjust to the younger child's maturity level and be accommodating or the younger one will need to rise up and learn how to assimilate with the older child.

In a person's life, this is typically how friendships begin. They are seeded in early childhood. This is not to neglect that later in life, other relationships can turn in to friendships and change roles. For example, in early childhood, a parent fills that role and not so much one as friend. However, in early adulthood, that role of parent can change and turn into one of friendship because the parenting stage is not as dominant or needed. A parent is always a parent for sure and the love and respect is one that can never change. However, the role changes like a caterpillar transforming into a beautiful butterfly.

There are modern changes in the meaning of friend. In some ways, I believe that this pollutes the definitional nucleus of what a friend is. For the first time in history, we have not only physical social circles, but we also have social media circles. On one platform, Facebook especially, a connection with another person is called a "friend." However, this friend can actually be a friend within the traditional definition, or it can just be someone that you really don't know but have a digital connection with. You can have friends that you never even communicate with. The interesting thing is that with a personal Facebook account, you can have up to 5,000 friends. Obviously, there is no practical way that you can have a traditional friendship with all 5,000 of these people.

There is a deeper meaning to what a true friend embodies. I believe the Bible to be God's Word to us and the source of answers to all the questions we could ever have. What does the Bible have to say about friendship? In this discussion about Biblical friendship, we will find that Abraham is at the front and center!

Abraham holds one title that no one else in the entire Bible held: Friend of God! Abraham is called Friend of God three times in the Bible. One of these times, he is affectionately called this by God Himself!

2 Chronicles 20:7 NKJV says, "*Are* You not our God, *who* drove out the inhabitants of this land before Your people Israel, and gave it to the descendants of <u>Abraham Your friend</u> forever? (underline mine)

Similarly, in James 2:23 NKJV, we read: "And the Scripture was fulfilled which says, "Abraham believed God, and it was accounted to him for righteousness." And he was called the <u>friend of God</u>." (underline mine)

God calls Abraham his friend in Isaiah 41:8 NKJV, "'But you, Israel, *are* My servant, Jacob whom I have chosen, The descendants of <u>Abraham My friend</u>.'" (underline mine)

So how did Abraham get this special title? How did he become God's friend?

I believe the real question is, "What is God's definition of friend?" Man can have so many varied definitions of what a friend is and what it means. These definitions are often not in alignment with what God has purposed the definition of friend. Instead of a definition that is based on emotion or what is beneficial for one person, we can look to God's unchanging definition instead of one that is relative, and changes based on something fleeting.

James 4:4 AMP says, "You adulteresses [disloyal sinners—flirting with the world and breaking your vow to God]! Do you not know that being the world's friend [that is, loving the things of the world] is being God's enemy? So, whoever chooses to be a friend of the world makes himself an enemy of God." There are key elements regarding the definition of friend in this verse.

One very obvious take away here is that we can be a friend of God, but we can also be an enemy of God. These two are at polar spectrums on the relationship scale. We can be one or the other. It seems to leave no middle ground. We are one or the other. If we are an enemy of God, we learn that we make that choice by loving the things of the world. We choose to be an enemy of God by being the world's friend. If we are the world's friend, then we are not a friend of God, but have chosen to be an enemy of God. Loving the things of the world may be outright loving the things of the world, but even flirting with the world has crossed the friendship line. On that side of the line, you are a friend of the world. It appears from this verse that we cannot be a friend of God if we are flirting with the world which is being disloyal to God. If we are disloyal to God, then we are called adulteresses, choosing the untrue in place of the true, looking in the face of the paramour instead of the face of the bridegroom.

In the life of Abraham, we see that during our introduction to Abraham (back when he was called Abram), God gave him an initial instruction to "Leave it all behind". (Genesis 12:1 TPT) Abram came from a place where the people were friends of the world. They not only flirted with the world, but they were committed to their relationship with the world. They were idol worshippers, making idols and worshipping them. They had made no vow to God to even break. They were all in, fully persuaded and loving this friendship with the enemy.

God knew that in order to take Abram to his destiny and fulfil his promise to Abram, there would need to be a change, a break, and a separation from this environment. The journey from Ur and also from Haran to the promised land set Abram apart from those of his past, those that chose friendship with the world and not friendship with God. God had in mind friendship with Abram. Friendship with God would facilitate the journey and pull in the promise.

When Abram left Haran, this is the start of a beautiful friendship with God, one that God defined Himself as friendship. Just as all friendships develop and mature, we see this happen between Abram and God throughout Abram's life. Proverbs 12:26 NKJV tells us, "The righteous should choose his friends carefully, For the way of the wicked leads them astray". We can either choose God or the world. We should follow this sage wisdom and do like Abram and choose God.

Proverbs 18:24 AMP elaborates on friendship: "The man of *too many* friends [chosen indiscriminately] will be broken in pieces *and* come to ruin, but there is a [true, loving] friend who [is reliable and] sticks closer than a brother". Here, we learn that if we choose to have too many friends, those friends are probably chosen indiscriminately. This person has not chosen the people that he should have in his close circle of intimate relationships. Because these friends are not the appropriate choices, they will cause ruin and brokenness. I believe that upon examination of the meaning of this verse, we find that our close friends are not necessarily great in number. If they are, then we have most likely made an unwise decision to befriend them. However, friendship is reserved for a few intimate, specifically tailored for us, purposefully chosen by us and sent by God.

The more friends we allow in our inner circles, we risk tainting the intimacy and purity that is there. We walk close to the line and even cross over the boundary of flirting with the world by indiscriminately allowing relationships into our lives that should not be there. I believe that our friendships with other people and our choosing them to enter our circle should hinge on the status of their relationship with God.

One very special key from Proverbs 18:24 is that we find out that there is a true and loving friend who is reliable and will stick closer than a brother. Friends are human. Even the best have weaknesses. When we are disappointed by a friendship, we can be encouraged that there is a friend who will never disappoint. He is perfect, true, loyal, absolute love, and self-sacrificing. His name is Yahweh!

"A friend loves at all times." (Proverbs 17:17 AMP) Yahweh is the friend that sticks closer than any other friend. No matter if we fall short in our relationship with Him, He still loves us. He never stops loving us. He is the constant friend that never changes. He picks up the broken pieces we have dropped and puts them back together. He fulfills his end of the covenant even when we fail. This is the nature of who God is: He is Love! "The one who does not love has not become acquainted with God [does not and never did know Him], for God is love. [He is the originator of love, and it is an enduring attribute of His nature.]" (I John 4:8 AMP)

There is a powerful example of God stepping in for himself and for Abram to ensure that His perfect plan would be fulfilled for Abram. Abram has been following God and obeying God, waiting on the promise for years. He is patiently waiting for a son to fulfil the promise of God. Abram has a place in his heart that is yet to be filled and he has carved out for this son of promise. Abram has been highly blessed and favored and has accumulated great wealth. However, Abram knows that his is already an old man and without a son, this lifetime of wealth will go to his servant, Eliezer.

Abram shares his heart with God about how he passionately wants a son, one that is of his own body, one that he can make his sole beneficiary of this untold wealth. Abram was not afraid to share his desires with God. He had a relationship that was close and intimate with Yahweh. Abram did not feel guilty that he was talking to Yahweh about this unfulfilled promise from God. God assures Abram that he will have a son from his own body. Abram's own biological son is to be his heir, not Abram's servant. God instructs Abram to bring a heifer, a female goat, a ram, turtledove and a young pigeon and sacrifice them. Abram cut all the animals except the birds in two and laid each half opposite the other in two rows.

Abram stood by his sacrifices and drove vultures away that came down to try and interfere and steal the sacrifices. At this point, Abram went into a deep state of sleep and God spoke to him, telling him about his descendants and how they would be held as slaves in a foreign country, but that God would bring them back out of slavery to the promised land.

When the sun had set and it was very dark, there suddenly appeared a smoking firepot and a blazing torch that passed between the carcasses. Yahweh entered into covenant with Abram promising the land to Abram and giving the metes and bounds of the property. The smoking firepot points us to the Father and the blazing torch points us to the Son, Jesus. In the ancient Near East, it was the custom to light a torch or a lamp when making a covenant. This symbolized that the fire of destruction would come if the covenant were to be broken. Here, God's promise or covenant to Abram which He spoke to Abram that very night became the "title deed" to the land. Yahweh warranted and gave clear title to Abram in perpetuity, to his descendants forever.[41]

An interesting thing happened when the blazing torch and the smoking firepot passed through the two portions of the sacrifices. In a covenant agreement, it would have been typical for the two parties – Abram and Yahweh – to pass through the meat pieces together. This would have solidified their responsibilities and to uphold the agreement they made with each other. However, something significant happened here. Only one party to the covenant passed between the two portions of sacrifices: God Himself! Yahweh passed for Himself, but also for his friend Abram as well. God made it impossible for Abram's misdeeds to stop or prevent His perfect plan for Abram!

God really did fill in the gap for Abram in a way that no human could do. God shows Abram that he is sticking by his side closer than a brother. This act and gesture of God, showing Abram his love and commitment, His ability to do for Abram what Abram cannot do for himself, elevated their friendship to a new level. This deepened their relationship, and it became more intimate. Abram is experiencing God at greater levels and on terms he has not yet seen or experienced.

Abram's friendship with God continues to deepen and become more intimate as they continue the journey together. Although Abram is not perfect, God is and He never changes. We have just discovered how

God stepped in where Abram could not and solidified the covenant. God Himself passed between the meat portions of the sacrifices. God is leading Abram to a new revelation of true friendship – to lay down his own life for his friends. John 15:13-15 AMP: "No one has greater love [nor stronger commitment] than to lay down his own life for his friends. You are my friends if you keep on doing what I command you. I do not call you servants any longer, for the servant does not know what his master is doing; but I have called you [My] friends, because I have revealed to you everything that I have heard from My Father."

In this passage, there are several keys that I will point out and discuss as it relates to friendship. The obvious is that a true friend is self-sacrificing. We have just seen God pass through the sacrifices for Himself and Abram. However, God will do this again and this act points prophetically to Jesus being the ultimate sacrifice for all mankind. Jesus, a descendant of Abram, will eventually come as fully God and fully man, to be the sacrifice that man cannot make to ever bring the two halves back together. The separation that sin has caused has left a gap between God and man that no lesser sacrifice can cover up or take away. God will send His Son, Jesus, to stand in that gap and bring the two halves back together.

Although Abram perhaps did not understand the full prophetic significance, I do believe that Abram understood what was to come. Abraham (as he was later called) acted out his own prophetic self-sacrifice at Mount Moriah in the binding of Isaac.

When Abram had this encounter with Yahweh, after Abram expressed his continued desire for his own son and that this promised son would be his sole heir, God took him outside of his tent and told him to gaze into the sky and see all the stars. God told him to try and count the stars. If Abram could grasp the magnitude of the number of stars which are countless, then he would have a vision of the magnitude of the promise of descendants. God told Abram, "Your seed will be as numerous as the stars" (Genesis 15:5 TPT)! The very next verse is significant. "And Abram trusted every word Yahweh had spoken! And because of his faith, Yahweh credited it to him as righteousness." (Genesis 15:6 TPT) This is the very verse that is quoted in James 2:23 (one of the three times Abraham is called Friend of God).

Even though Abram was already 75 years old when God gave him the promise of a natural born son, Abram was now even older. Sarai was also older and in the natural so far beyond in any way possible being able to be a mother. She was decades past being able to conceive children. Beyond her age, the fact remains that even when she was of childbearing age, she had been barren. With so many impossible factors converging to show Abram the current status, the eyes of Abram were not turned toward the impossible but toward absolute belief in every word of God. Abram believed every single one of these words: "Your seed will be as numerous as the stars"! (Genesis 15:5 TPT) Abram trusted every word. Against all he could see with his eyes, Abram had eyes of faith.

"And the Scripture was fulfilled which says, 'Abraham believed God, and it was accounted to him for righteousness.' And he was called the friend of God." (James 2:23 NKJV) Abraham became vested with the title "Friend of God" because he believed every word of God. Abraham trusted God's word, the intimate conversation and promise of God above what he saw, what others said, even above what Sarai may have said to Abraham.

Abraham's belief in God was credited into Abraham's account and he was made right before God. He could stand before God and look him in the face and speak to him as a friend. Abraham's friendship was evident in his intimacy with God and the way he believed God's every word.

Abraham had fallen in love with God. This love for God was returned because God was always in love with Abraham. In James 2:23, the Greek text is often translated as "friend of God," the Greek word *philos* can be used or translated as the love that bonds friends together.[42]

We are God's friends if we do what God commands us to do. This is another key which we can glean from John 15:13-15. To refresh, it says, "No one has greater love [nor stronger commitment] than to lay down his own life for his friends. You are my friends if you keep on doing what I command you. I do not call you servants any longer, for the servant does not know what his master is doing; but I have called you [My] friends, because I have revealed to you everything that I have heard from My Father." (John 15:13-15 AMP)

When God commands or instructs us to do something, we should obey. We see Abraham doing this over and over in his life. We see this first when Abram follows God's instruction to leave Haran and journey to the land of promise, leaving everything behind. We see it over and over again, even when it goes against what looks like it is contradictory to God's promise. When God tells Abraham to sacrifice Isaac, his only son, the one he had waited on for decades. Yet, Abraham immediately said "Yes" to God and made preparations to leave to go to Mount Moriah early the next morning. Abraham kept on doing what God commanded him.

One of Abram's concerns was that Eliezer, his servant would be his heir. This passage in John is beautiful because it takes us from servant to friend. Abram was stuck in a place where Eliezer was the one who would receive the inheritance. Yet, this was not God's plan! Because of Abram's obedience over and over, he went from a place of Eliezer to a place of Isaac. He went from a place where he did not know what God was doing to a place where God communicated his thoughts to Abraham. God reveals everything when we choose Him as a friend. He communicates his thoughts and intentions.

There is an event which happens later in Abraham's life in which he is visited by three men. These three men who visit are really two angels and Yahweh. Abraham recognizes them immediately and I believe he knew who they were. Once Abraham sees them, he immediately goes to them and tells them he will prepare a lavish feast for them so they will be well fed and nourished. Abraham has Sarah quickly begin to prepare fresh bread and he has his servant prepare his choice tender calf for his guests. We see a picture of friendship here. Abraham is entertaining Yahweh and going above and beyond what is a normal meal preparation. He is bringing out his best for his friend.

During this time of resting, foot washing, and being honored by the presence of his friend, Abraham enjoys the conversation and the time together of fellowship and just being together. God personally came to visit Abraham and to tell him again that Sarah will have the promised son in one year. I believe that because of their bond of friendship, Yahweh wanted to personally visit Abraham to tell him the time had come. What a wonderful surprise to be visited by God and be told that the time of waiting was almost over. The promise was about to be conceived and born. Not only did God come, but he brought two companions, two angels to be part of the time together.

When it was time for God to leave, Abraham walked with him. He didn't just walk to the end of the tent grounds; he walked all the way to the overlook to where they could see the city of Sodom below. They talked the entire time. Even though God had other business to take care of, the two still wanted to savor the last minutes of being together.

This reminds me of how we leave someone's home in the South. When it is time to leave, we tell each other "bye" and then we walk them to the door. Then we say "bye" again. Then we hug and then we walk them out to the car and talk some more. Then we say "bye" and then we open their car door and then we hug again and tell each other "bye" again. Then as they leave, they roll down the window and we tell them to call when they get home, so we know they got there safely.

Just as much as Abraham enjoyed God's company, God enjoyed Abraham's as well. In fact, because of their friendship, God said, "Should I really hide from Abraham what I intend to do? After all, he will become a great and powerful nation, and every nation on earth will be blessed through him.

It is true: I have singled him out as my own, so that he will lead his family and household to follow my ways and live by what is right and just. I will fulfill all the promises that I have spoken to him". (Genesis 18:17-19 TPT) God wanted to share what he was about to do with Abraham. I believe that God wanted Abraham's thoughts about the situation in Sodom. That is how friends communicate. They share. They talk. They discuss. They tell each other the truth and what is on their heart.

So, Yahweh explained to Abraham that the outcry from all the injustice in Sodom was so great that He had to visit the city to assess the wickedness. Yahweh paused when they had reached the end of their destination together, giving Abraham time to respond. Then Abraham did something bold.

"Abraham came forward *to present his case* before Yahweh." (Genesis 18:23 TPT) If Abraham did not have an intimate relationship with

Yahweh, he would not have felt comfortable doing this. However, he did what a friend would do and gave Yahweh his thoughts about judgment and destruction of Sodom. He wanted to change God's mind and pleaded, "Are you really going to sweep away the righteous while you judge the wicked" (Genesis 18:23 TPT)?

Abraham proceeded to ask if God would spare the city if 50 righteous people could be found. God answered Abraham and indicated that he would spare the city if 50 righteous were round. We know the story here. Abraham then asks the same question over and over and lowers the number each time, finally ending with ten people. God answers and tells Abraham that he will spare the city for the sake of only ten righteous. Abraham was interceding for the people of Sodom, specifically, his nephew Lot and his family. However, there is something deeper than intercession here. There is friendship. There was love for each other. There was *philos* as the basis of their friendship – love that bonded Abraham and Yahweh together. In Genesis 19:20 TPT, it says, "So before God destroyed the cities of the plain where Lot had settled, he remembered *his affection* for Abraham and spared Lot from all the destruction".

There is a song which has been made popular by the group, "Phillips Craig & Dean" called "Friend of God". It was written by Israel Houghton and Michael Gungor. The lyrics in verse 1 and verse 2 are:

Who am I that You are mindful of me that You hear me when I call
Is it true that You are thinking of me, How You love me it's amazing
I am a friend of God, I am a friend of God

I am a friend of God, He calls me friend

Who am I that You are mindful of me that you hear me when I call
Is it true that You are thinking of me how You love me

It's amazing, so amazing, it's amazing

It is amazing that we are loved so much by God. We are His creation and made in His image. It is something to comprehend that Yahweh, being who He is, being all sufficient, would want us to be His friend. God is mindful of us. He was mindful of Abraham. He took Abraham from a past that was going nowhere good and took him on a journey of faith. Along the way, an irreplaceable relationship developed and grew into something very beautiful. Abraham came to know God in a way that he had not before. He became God's friend. It is amazing that twice in the Bible, Abraham is called Friend of God by others. However, even more remarkable and precious is that God said that Abraham was His friend. Like Abraham, I too, want God to call me His friend. The Chorus and Bridge of "Friend Of God" says it in an unparalleled way:

I am a friend of God, I am a friend of God I am a friend of God, He calls me friend.

I am a friend of God, I am a friend of God I am a friend of God, He calls me friend.

God Almighty, Lord of Glory, you have called me friend God Almighty, Lord of Glory, You have called me friend God Almighty, Lord of Glory, You have called me friend.

CHAPTER 9

Name change: Abram to Abraham

What is in a name? If you are a parent, you know just how challenging it is to name a baby. Sometimes you spend months picking out names and then narrowing them down because you want to choose the perfect one. This is something your child has no control over. Once you name the child, that is his or her name for life. I have met people who absolutely despised their names. And to be honest, they did have a terrible sounding name. Other people are very pleased and content with their names.

Names are chosen for a variety of reasons. It is very common for first born boys to be named after their father or grandfather. I see a lot of girls with the middle name of their mother. Some people have names that have a particular meaning. For example, my name, Crystal, means "brilliantly clear and pure," "ice," "a transparent Quartz gemstone, usually colorless, that can be cut to reflect brilliant light." Crystal also means "follower of Christ".

During different periods of time, names can dominate and then be less used. We see this in different generations of people. The names of our grandparents' generation were in some ways different than some we see being given today. There are also very trendy names that have never been used in previous generations that we see more of today.

The purpose behind the name choice is different for everyone. However, the similarity for all people is that everyone does have a name. Although some do not understand or recognize the significance of the name they choose or are given, the Bible is clear that what is in a name is very powerful and extremely significant.

A name is a word packed and infused with powerful prophetic implications over a person (and sometimes a thing), their life, purpose, and destiny. The first time we see a word being spoken is in the creation account. "And God said, 'Let there be light; and there was light.'" (Genesis 1:3 AMP) This is the first time God spoke. Before God spoke, there was no light. It had never existed before. Then, when the words came from the mouth of God, His words spoke forth and created the thing that had never existed. That thing God imagined and spoke into existence became the word He called it. He called it light and out of nothing but through his spoken word, that thing became what God called it to be.

I like the Passion Translation version of this verse. It says, "And then God announced: 'Let there be light,' and light burst forth" (Genesis 1:3 TPT)! God not only spoke the word, he announced to all the universe that this thing which had never been was about to be and it obeyed; light burst forth and submitted to the authority in the word being spoken and boldly announced for the tiniest atom to the largest galaxy to hear! Light didn't just slowly take time to appear. It obeyed the word and the DNA instructions packed within the meaning and sound of that spoken word burst forth into creation.

God never speaks a word that is contrary to his character. The psalmist says to God, "You are good and *and* kind and do good..." (Psalm 119:68 AMP). Therefore, any word He speaks brings forth something that is also going to align with His character. "And God saw that the light was good (suitable, pleasant) *and* He approved it..." (Genesis 1:4 AMP) So God named the thing he imagined "light" and spoke that name. Inherent in that name and in speaking that name were the irreversible and absolute creation instructions for this thing that embodied and burst forth the very meaning of the name "light."

Light became light. Light did not become anything else. The instructions in the word "light" were just for that very thing – light. God had to speak another word, another name to bring forth the firmament or the expanse of the sky. This was the second time God spoke a name. "And God said, Let there be a firmament [the expanse of the sky] in the midst of the waters…" (Genesis 1:6 AMP) The firmament became the dome between the waters to separate the water above from the water below. (Genesis 1:6 TPT) The name "firmament" came into existence with the spoken word of God. The firmament had never existed before God's spoken word for it to come into being. The coded instructions in the name "firmament" created just that, the dome or the atmosphere around the earth. It did not create the moon or the stars. Those would come with instructions encoded for those specific things – DNA instructions in the words "moon" and stars."

Names have invisible instructions that are coded and packed within the meaning of that name. Those instructions act like DNA for the name. They give the thing or person it attaches to a prophetic direction. There is an invisible spiraling ladder with tightly woven rungs of encoded prophetic information about what that name is to become, the boundaries of what it is to be and not to be, and the future potential of that thing or person. So far, we have seen a few examples of that in the names that God spoke forth in the creation account. Light became that very thing – light. The firmament became exactly that – firmament.

A good illustration of the meaning of names, their exact meaning, boundaries, and potential would be the difference between a tide and a flood. Both have to do with water and not only water, but in general, large amounts of water. However, a tide is regulated and has boundaries. There is a minimum level of water and there is a maximum level of water. The tide never oversteps its boundaries, even though it is constantly coming in and going out. The definitional nature of tide is water that is constantly changing but only within its preset boundaries. However, a flood is water that overflows given boundaries and invades surrounding areas. A flood has no limit for its maximum water level.

When the tide is coming in, we would never say it is flooding because that is not the meaning of flood. The encoded meaning and prophetic potential in the names "tide" and "flood" are different. They describe different situations with water, but they are clearly different. This is why we use the name of each word to call the different situations what they are. We are in effect describing the situation and at the same time aligning with the prophetic instructions packed in those names.

In the creation account, God did not speak forth once or twice to fully create and bring forth creation to its fullest potential within his imagination. God spoke ten times in the creation story. These can be called the Ten Commandments of creation.[43]

I believe this is significant as it relates to how God uses numbers to illustrate and gives us additional revelation and insight into something. God imagined the universe with all the galaxies, the stars, the planets. He conceived in His mind the atmosphere to cover the earth, the lush vegetation and animals of striking beauty and variety. God's heart held his ultimate creation, man, and the love relationship He desired with him. The fullness and wholeness of the vision God had for creation was epic. It was ultimate and complete. Yet, God didn't create it all in one word. He spoke each part into existence, creating it in steps and with order. He spoke ten times with the tenth bringing it to wholeness and completion.

The number ten prophetically means complete, completion of an order or cycle, full, and with compete instructions.[44]

"This number has to do with timelines and how God carries out a plan in perfect order. It's the number where God reveals His plan and sets things in order according to that plan. One of the four 'perfect' numbers, 10 has to do with God setting things up for His purpose."[45]

We see that the 10 names God spoke forth in creating his masterpiece brought forth fullness and those were the complete instructions. God created and brought the purpose about through order in ten steps - ten names – all with their own separately coded DNA instructions for fulfillment.

In part 1 of this book, we went examined the encounters that Abraham had with God in minute detail. The very interesting and uncoincidental factor is that Abraham had ten encounters with God where God spoke to Abraham. He spoke words and prophetic destiny over Abraham. Abraham is a masterpiece in the making, just like God spoke and created the universe. He encountered Abraham ten times and in this orderly process, he spoke words to Abraham that brought about fulfillment, wholeness, and destiny.

Just as God took 7 days in creation and did not speak all the instructions at once, it took about 25 years of a step by step, orderly process for Abraham to ultimately be where God destined him to be. Each encounter with God brought Abraham a step further and encoded him with more prophetic DNA about his future and the promise to him. With each word spoken over and to Abraham, the words began to unfold their purpose in him and take on the meaning of the words of promise and fulfillment.

All the words God spoke to Abraham were important and launched him into a new level, each time getting him closer to wholeness and fulfillment. However, there is a unique and significant word that was spoken to him in his sixth encounter with God. Abram had been his name since birth. Abram is now 99 years old. He is almost a centenarian. That is quite an accomplishment, even in his day with people having longer life spans. Abram has had a full life in his 99 years, but he hasn't quite seen fulfillment. There is a difference, and the elevating factor is about to be spoken to Abram.

Abram means "exalted father". The Hebrew for Abram is 'avram. The "av" means "father." This is very similar to the name Abiram where the Hebrew would be 'aviram. Names that have the "Abi" "at the beginning have a similar meaning which is "the father is."[46]

For 99 years, the man we know to be the Father of our Faith, was called Abram or "exalted father". When someone called him by his name, they were speaking the prophetic DNA encoded instructions that are inherent in the name "Abram" over him. Over and over, Abram was called "exalted father." The spoken name over him could not help but coming to pass, in bursting forth at some point in his life. When Abram (alias "exalted father") was 86 years old, the encoded instructions burst forth with the birth of Ishmael. Even though Ishmael was not the promised son, he did technically fulfill the boundaries and potential of what was encoded in the name "Abram." Abram did see himself become an exalted father. However, this was not the ideal and ultimate (or even correct) fulfillment of what God really had in mind for Abram.

In order to outgrow the boundaries of the definition of Abram, God would have to give him a new name which would have greater potential and much larger boundaries. The boundaries of Abram cannot fit all the stars in the sky. The vision for his life was too big and Abram needed a new name with new instructions embedded for prophetic fulfillment.

Before God gives Abram a new name, I absolutely love the fact that God reveals to Abram one of His names as a precursor to what He is about to do! After 13 years of silence and no encounters from God, something powerful is about to take place. God passionately tells Abram "I am the God who is more than enough" (Genesis 17:1 TPT). For the man who has been hoping against all hope, hanging in there when all the world looks like it is against the promise of God, and year after year of seeing nothing as it relates to a promised son, God loudly and boldly tells Abram that He is the God who is more than enough. God is more than enough for his history, for Sarai's years of barrenness, and even for the odds of being decades past the time when a fertile wife would conceive and have a child. God is not just enough. He is not just equal to what we need or what He has promised. He is more than enough. There is surplus and abundance and overflow attached to the meaning of His name.

God is El Shaddai. El is one of the words used for God. God is equal to El Shaddai. They are one in the same. The meaning of El Shaddai is encoded in this name of God. The DNA instructions cannot change the meaning or who He is. This name of God means "God of the Holy Mountain," "God of the Wilderness," "God the Destroyer of Enemies," "God the All-Sufficient One," "God the Nurturer of Babies (the Breasted One)," "God the Almighty," "the Sovereign God," and "God who is more than enough!"[47]

God is full of compassion for Abram and watching over his promise to fulfill it in Abram's life. To Abram, who is 99 years old and who is still contending for the promise of God, this is a powerful reminder and comfort to him that God is who He says He is and that He is more than enough to not only be sufficient for Abram, but to be more than enough for him.

God is and has been with Abram through the physical wilderness of traveling from the place of Ur and Haran to the promised land. He has been with Abram in his combat endeavors to rescue Lot, and he has destroyed every enemy of Abram even when Abram fell short. God is the All-Sufficient One. He is sufficient within himself. He needs no one or nothing. He has enough to provide and He will provide to over sufficiency. He will imagine the vision and name it so that it will be fulfilled. And because God is good, what he speaks forth and creates is always good. It aligns with his character.

God is the Nurturer of Babies. This is powerful as well because I believe God is telling Abram that his promised son is already in his imagination and He is nurturing little Isaac even now before his birth and He has Isaac's destiny on high alert before all of heaven and earth. He is the Sovereign God and His word will not return void, useless, or without result. (Isaiah 55:11 AMP)

After God revealed to Abram that he is El Shaddai and all that is prophetically encoded in his name, God shows off to Abram just how He can in a moment, elevate him to a new level with a new status and expanded boundaries for prophetic achievement. While Abram was on his face in awe before God, God said to him, "I establish my covenant with you: 'You will become a father of many nations. You will no longer be named Abram *because I am changing your name to Abraham, for I have made you a father of many nations.*'" (Genesis 17:3-5 TPT)

No longer will this man of destiny be called "exalted father." He will now be launched into destiny with the name "father of a multitude" or "father of many nations." With this new name, "Abraham," will come a new set of prophetic DNA instructions with enlarged boundaries that are extensive enough to cover the massive promise. Just like the definition of tide has a minimum and maximum capacity, Abram has been living within the capacity of that old name. However, a flood is coming with all the prophetic implications of the new name Abraham. The definitional measures of "Abraham" cannot be contained and there is not only going to be a crossing over of previous boundaries, but a surge and a taking over the land that will be a blessing to the entire earth. As with the food of Noah, the blessing God will pour over Abraham and his descendants until they do in fact become as numerous as the stars in the sky and the sand on the seashore.

The word for father in Hebrew again is "'av" which is an ancestor, whether immediate or remote, as in "father of many nations." The Greek word for father is "pater." This leads us to the name patriarch, which we know to be the father of a family, tribe, or race. Abraham will become known as the Patriarch, not only of the Jewish people, but of our Faith. The "im" suffix on the end of Abraham [Abram + im] makes the meaning change from singular to plural. So, Abraham is father of a multitude and signifies nations, tribes, cities, and towns rather than individuals.[48]

In Proverbs, Solomon gives some very sage and powerful wisdom regarding the word. He says that the word will be life to your inner self or to your soul (Proverbs 3:22 AMP). Names are words that we speak. Those names can be life giving. If a name is given by God, it is by its definition and character life giving and destiny promoting!

Again, Solomon has some words of wisdom and tells us that the tongue of the wise brings healing (Proverbs 12:18 AMP). The words we speak and the names we are called bring life or death. This is because "A man's belly shall be satisfied with the fruit of his mouth; and with the increase of his lips shall he be filled. Death and life are in the power of the tongue; and they that love it shall eat the fruit thereof" (Proverbs 18:20-21 KJV). What we speak and the words we use have life or death as consequences. God in his goodness and all-sufficiency and being more than enough, spoke life and promise and destiny over Abram when he changed his name and called him Abraham.

Now instead of just being called "exalted father" and being always pulled back from the high tide to the low tide of its destiny, he is called "father of a multitude". This new name shifts the destiny and the even the ability of the promise to come to pass. It is the right time for this upshift in Abraham's life. God has been with him through the journey, has seen his maturity and faithfulness come into a ripened state and the time is at hand for the promise to become reality.

Not only did God change Abraham's name, but God did the same wonderful thing for Sarai in the same encounter. In the case of Sarai, her name change to "Sarah" both basically mean "princess or woman of strength." It is believed that Sarai is simply the possessive form of Sarah, meaning "My Sarah." So, Sarah signifies her strength does not belong exclusively to her immediate family, but to the future nation of Israel and even the word at-large.[49]

Now, Sarah, even though she has been barren her entire life and is also decades past childbearing age is given a new name which is attached to the promise of God to Abraham. Sarah will indeed become the mother of the promised son, Isaac. She is not only a princess, but she is a woman of strength. Her strength doesn't come from the natural realm, but from the Lord. She is given a supernatural strength to conceive and bear a child even in her old age. Sarah is known for her supernatural youth and beauty. Now, she will also be known for her supernatural ability to become a mother of the Jewish people. Her strength helps to bring to pass the fulfillment of Isaac as well as the future descendants who will bring a blessing to the entire world.

Interestingly, the Hebrew word for "prince" is *sar*, which is formed from two Hebrew root words. There is a verb that means "to wrestle or to fight" and another verb which means "to rule or to govern (as royalty). Combining these two verbs gives us the Hebrew word *sar* and means "warring prince." Sarah is the feminine version of Sar. In this way, Sarah means "a princess who is a warrior".[50] Sarah certainly is a beautiful and supernaturally youthful princess who becomes the Matriarch of the Jewish people. She is the princess who is a warrior. With her supernatural infusion of strength, she conquers the battle of barrenness even in old age to become the mother of Isaac, the promised son.

A name change for both Abram and Sarai to Abraham and Sarah gives each of them not only a new name, but a new meaning, a redefined purpose, and the expanded boundaries to fulfill the promise of God for their lives.

In our society, typically when a woman gets married, she will take the last name of her husband. This name change signifies a newness, an unparalleled life transition, and new boundaries. She gains the name of her husband and with that is even sometimes referred to as Mrs. John Doe or Mrs. Doe. The privileges that her husband has, she now receives. The protection that her husband has, she now benefits from. She gains his family as her family. She gains the ability to go from a single lady to a married lady and possibly a mother. Her name change has benefits attached to it. The ultimate purpose for this name change is or should be love.

Love was also the purpose behind God changing the names of Abraham and Sarah. There was newness, a life-giving element, and combustion for destiny to burst forth because of all the embedded DNA instructions in their new names. El Shaddai in His love gave Abraham and

Sarah a new code and a new level and ability for His promise to be fulfilled in their lives.

We see other examples of God changing someone's name in the Bible. Some of these are:

- Jacob, meaning "caught by the heel" TO Israel, meaning "God may prevail/he struggles with God/God preserves"
- Saul, meaning "prayed for" TO Paul, meaning "small/humble"
- Simon, meaning "he has heard" TO Peter, meaning "the rock"

- Joseph, meaning "He will add" TO Barnabas, meaning "son of encouragement"

These are a few of the people whose name was changed by God. Each time their names were changes, their destinies were shifted closer into reality. The meaning of the names came into existence in the lives of each of these people. The people, more accurately, became the meaning of the name. Each person was pushed further into the position they needed to be in for their calling and purpose. Their inner self changed and aligned with the maturity level required to sustain the promise in their lives.

I told you earlier in this chapter the meaning of my name, Crystal, means "brilliantly clear and pure," "ice," "a transparent Quartz gemstone, usually colorless, that can be cut to reflect brilliant light". My name also means "follower of Christ". This really is very accurate about my personality and character and heart. For anyone who really knows me, I believe they would agree as well. For my entire life, I have been called "Crystal." I have been called "pure, and brilliantly clear". I have been called "follower of Christ". Those words, the meaning of the name, and the prophetic DNA instructions have been spoken over me every day, multiple times a day, for my entire life. The words bring forth what is spoken. I have become what the encoded instructions have proclaimed.

As we see in the name change of Abraham and Sarah, God is a proponent of changing someone's name. He is an advocate of increasing one's capacity for destiny and for giving us a new identity. The best and ultimate example of a name change is when we come to Christ. I believe that every name change in the Bible can only point us to Jesus. From Abram to Abraham and Sarai to Sarah and every other, God wants to show us how he can change us and transform us from what was to what He wants for us. God wants to show us how He can shape us and mold us into what he has imagined us to be. Before He knitted us and formed us in our mother's womb, He had already imagined us in His mind. "Before I formed you in the womb I knew *and* approved of you [as my chosen instrument], and before you were born, I separated *and* set you apart, consecrating you; [and] appointed you as a prophet to the nations." (Jeremiah 1:5 AMP)

Just as God shared this touching and personal story of how He knew Jeremiah even before he was conceived, God had the same personal and intimate vision of each of us. He saw us and He knew our end from our beginning. He knows that where we begin in life isn't where He has in mind for our end. Just like when God spoke the word in the creation account, He named the thing He imagined, and it came forth when God spoke the word. God did this in increments and not all at once. Just like with Abram in his journey to becoming Abraham and Sarai to transitioning into the person of Sarai, we too, are on a journey from where we have been to where God has imagined us to be.

God even gave Adam the authority and ability to name each animal. Adam gave each species its Hebrew name. These weren't random names that Adam just casually thought of and chose. "According to the Kabbalah, the name of every creation is its life-source. The Hebrew letters carry a G-dly power, and, when put together in different formations, they give life wherever they are applied. Thus, all created things are directly affected by their Hebrew names, and the letters of which they are composed.

Here is a quote from the Midrash to Genesis 2:19:

When the Holy One, blessed be He, was about to create humankind, He consulted with His ministering angels, saying, "Let us make Adam." The angels responded, "What's so wonderful about this Adam?" So, He brought each creature before the angels and asked them, "This creature, what is its name?" But they did not know. Then He brought the creatures before Adam and asked him, "This creature, what is its name?" To which Adam responded, "This is shor [Hebrew for ox], this is chamor [donkey]…".

Adam was able to perceive the spiritual components of the creative spirit that brought every animal into being and named each animal in conjunction with its spiritual configuration."[51]

Adam named all the animals and perceived its spiritual makeup and destiny, boundaries, and parameters and in doing so, named the animal to be the very thing it was created to be. There is a marked difference and distinction and a celebration of the uniqueness between an ox and a donkey. Naming this one a "shor" and this one a "chamor" marked each of these animals for their own particular and set apart purpose and destiny.

I recently read about a town on the island of Anglesey, Wales, with one of the longest names known in the English language. It is the wonderful and quaint village named…

Llanfairpwllgwyngyllgogerychwyrndrobwlllantysiliogogogoch.

This was a bit of a chore to type! Even its shorter name is cumbersome: Llanfairpwllgwyngyll. However, aside from the phonics test this presents, I really want to share with you how the meaning of the name aligns with what we have been discussing in this chapter. The meaning of this town's name is "The Church of St. Mary in a hollow of white hazel, near to the rapid whirlpool, and to St. Tisilio Church, near to a red cave." However this English name came into being, this is significant because its meaning is very descriptive of the purpose and destiny of the town as well as to its boundaries. The meaning is the DNA encoded instructions for this very long name.[52]

Clearly, the name of something or someone is extremely significant and marks that thing or person for purpose and destiny. A name change also marks a transition and elevation point in the purpose or destiny as well as the capacity of that thing or person to fulfill all its creation potential. The changing by God of Abraham and Sarah's name represented a change in their lives, both in the eyes of God and in society just as this takes place when a woman takes her husband's last name in marriage.

Again, all this points us to Jesus. Jesus has a name which is above every name! Philippians 2:9-10 KJV tells us, "Wherefore God also hath highly exalted him, and given him a name which is above every name: That at the name of Jesus every knee should bow, of things in heaven, and things in earth, and things under the earth." Jesus' name is the highest name in all the universe. Any other name must bow to his majestic and holy name.

In this name is encoded the DNA instructions of power and authority, salvation, and all The Blessing of God. Because Jesus defeated death and every curse with a total blowout victory against satan and his allies, this name now carries all the backing of heaven. When we accept Jesus and make Him the Lord of our life, we also gain the privilege of having His name as our name. Just as a wife takes her husband's name and then is covered with all the benefits of his name, we take on the overflow of benefits and blessings that are inherent in the name of Jesus. The Bible tells us that we, the church, are His Bride. Because of this pure and absolute love, we want to take His name. Not just because it is beautiful and altogether lovely, but also because it is the name that is above all others. Jesus, our Bridegroom, is waiting to cover us with the love and benefits and protection of His name.

This is the most profound and the pinnacle of all name changes. When God imagined us, He had exponential destiny and beauty and purpose for us. He loves us too much to leave us as we are without taking us to that ultimate end. "And I am convinced *and* sure of this very thing, that He Who began a good work in you will continue until the day of Jesus Christ [right up to the time of His return], developing [that good work] *and* perfecting *and* bringing it to full completion in you." (Philippians 1:6 AMP) God loves us too much to leave us without his divine completion in our lives. He desires us to go from our old name to His name. This name change changes the DNA structure of our purpose and destiny. The embedded code in His name is pure and without any defect. When we take His name, we gain everything that He is and everything He has. This is the ultimate life altering, destiny accessing change we could ever have or experience.

It gets better. Not only do we get to take the name of Jesus, there are more precious and intimate name changes that only Jesus will give to those that overcome. In Revelation 2:17, we find out that Jesus will "give him a shining white stone. And written upon the white stone is inscribed his new name, known only to the one who receives it." Because of the intimate love that our Bridegroom has for us, there are personal mysteries that are imparted to us. These are intimate secrets between us and Jesus. Only the person who is given the stone with the new name knows the name written on it.[53] A chapter later, we discover that Jesus will write on us the name of His God and the name of the city of His God – the New Jerusalem. Jesus will also write His own name on us (Revelation 3:12 TPT)!

The names that Jesus will bestow on us includes a new name known only by us, the name of God, the name of Jerusalem, and Jesus' new name. This is exciting! This is life changing. Life doesn't have to be stale and stagnant, just existing and slowly but patiently giving up hope for the future God has put inside of you. The nudgings and promptings are evidence of the already encoded potential inside you for God's purpose and destiny that is unique to just you. The only way to reach the completeness is by a name change. This is not just any name change, but by taking the name of Jesus!

For us as believers in Jesus, this is the pinnacle. Just as God changed Abraham and Sarah's name to give them a new identity, a new coded DNA full of new life-giving instructions, we receive the ultimate name change by taking Jesus' name – our Lord, our King, our Savior, and most intimately, our Bridegroom!

CHAPTER 10

The Father's Blessing – Clearing and unlocking pathways for destiny

In the last chapter, we discussed the prophetic DNA embedded in a name and the powerful and life altering destiny shift that occurs in a name change. In this chapter, we will discuss the prophetic significance and the DNA destiny shifters that are embedded in the power of the Father's spoken blessing. When the Father's blessing is spoken over a child, this does something unprecedented in the spirit and life of that child by clearing and unlocking pathways for that child's destiny.

The greatest blessing one can receive is the blessing of the Father. God created us with a need to be loved. Within that need for love is a deeper need for intimacy. That need to be loved creates a vacuum which causes people to seek love in others until it is filled in the love of our Father.

In the very beginning, when God created Adam and Eve, one of the first things He did was bless them. Before God sent Adam and Eve out on their journey to reach their life's purpose, He blessed them. This is the very first blessing and this blessing encompasses God's overarching scope of blessing for all mankind, then and now. We can call this the Blessing. Every other blessing will fall within this initial blessing upon God's ultimate masterpiece – mankind.

The very first action God took after creating Adam and Eve was to invoke His blessing upon them. Genesis 1:27 KV tells us, "So God created man in his own image, in the image of God created he him;

male and female created he them." The very next verse invokes the blessing. There is no pause, no gap, and no break. Immediately after God created them, verse 28 says "And God blessed them…"

I like how the Passion Translation describes the blessing that God spoke over them. "And God blessed them *in his love,* saying: 'Reproduce and be fruitful! Populate the earth and subdue it! Reign over the fish of the sea, the birds of the air, and every creature that lives on earth.'" (Genesis 1:28 TPT) One reason I like this translation is because it emphasizes that God, as their Father, blessed them in his love! The blessing cannot be what it is apart from love.

We know that God is love. (I John 4:8 KJV) He is in His nature and character that very thing – Love. He is absolute Love. Therefore, the nature of God being Love is on display as a good Father loving his children and blessing them before they begin their work on earth to fulfill their purpose. The blessing is an act of great love from a loving Father.

God's blessing upon the human family clearly implies love. With this blessing, the Father is empowering Adam and Eve with an infusion of power and favor to succeed.[54] With this blessing, God can then send his children into the world to accomplish all He created them to be and achieve.

God placed Adam and Eve in the garden of Eden and gave them dominion over all the earth and the ability to subdue it and replenish it. He blessed his children with the ability to be fruitful and multiply. God gave his children everything. He gave them and made full provision to meet all their needs. There was no lack for Adam and Eve. Whatever God had destined them for, they had provision to get there. God gave to Adam and Eve freely and abundantly.

It is not in the nature of God as a loving Father to withhold from his children. God's original purpose for man can be seen here. God is a loving Father who gives freely to his children. They had not done anything at this point except be created by God. They did not have a track record or any good achievements or accolades. More importantly, they had not even made mistakes or disappointed God. The blessing was not a reward for their actions. The blessing was only motivated by God's heart of love for them.

Psalm 35:27 KJV tells us that God takes pleasure in us, his children. The psalmist also says later that God promised not to withhold any good thing from those who walk upright before Him (Psalm 84:11 KJV). In Psalm 37:4 KJV, God promised to those who set their hearts upon Him that he will give them the desires of their hearts. So, we see the loving nature of our Father here. He wants to give to his children even more than they need.

As human parents, we know just how much we love our children and want them to succeed. We want to give them provision and blessings and try to do this to the best of our ability. Even in our humanity, our desire is for the wellbeing and success of our children. How much more does God have this desire in his heart. Matthew 7:9-11 TPT illustrates this principle so well, "Do you know of any parent who would give his hungry child, who asked for food, a plate of rocks instead? Or when asked for a piece of fish, what parent would offer his child a snake instead? If you, imperfect as you are, know how to lovingly take care of your children and give them what's best, how much more ready is your heavenly Father to give wonderful gifts to those who ask him?"

God is a perfect Father. He is absolute Love. His provision is just what we need. His gifts to us and his blessing is perfect in every way. The Blessing He spoke over Adam and Eve was not merited in any way. It was a result of and demonstration of His great love for his children and their success. He didn't create them to just leave them just surviving in the dark. He created them and then blessed them to succeed – to fulfill the wonderful purpose and destiny He had imagined for them even before they were created.

The Hebrew word for bless is *barak*. This word occurs 330 times in the Bible. It means "to bestow good upon". It makes sense and is obvious that God's ultimate purpose even before the creation of man was to bless and prosper his ultimate masterpiece – mankind. The Greek word for bless is *eulogeo*. Similarly, this word means "to cause to prosper, to make happy, and to bestow blessings on." (The ultimate blessing was the gift God sent in Jesus to bless us through Him bringing us the fullness of the blessing – salvation. In Ephesians 1:3 KJV, we discover that we have been blessed with all spiritual blessings in Christ and have inherited the blessing of Abraham.

God spoke the blessing over Adam and Eve. We see the same thing happen for Abraham. God, as Father, spoke his blessings over Abraham. In fact, the blessings He spoke over Abraham were not outside the scope of the blessing over Adam and Eve, His original blessing for mankind. Every blessing you read about in the Bible are all part of the original blessing over Adam and Eve.

"Those BLESSINGS are all part of a whole. They are pieces of something bigger and more powerful than anything most of us have ever imagined. Like parts of a watch that work together as one, each of them – from the new birth, to healing, to prosperity, to the power gifts of the Holy Spirit – are all part of a single declaration made by God 6,000 years ago. They are all the result of one BLESSING – *THE* BLESSING!

The one BESSING God spoke over Adam and Eve in the Garden of Eden.

The one BLESSING recorded in Genesis 1:28 that set forth God's will for all mankind, for all time: *Be fruitful, and multiply, and replenish the earth, and subdue it: and have dominion…*

With that one BLESSING, God bestowed on the family of man

everything they would ever need to become all He created them to be and to do all He had destined them to do. He released the only BLESSING any of us would ever need...that first BLESSING eventually became THE BLESSING of Abraham. You'll track it down through the generations and see the amazing things that happened to all who received it. You'll get a clearer understanding of how THE BLESSING empowered the true Seed of Abraham, The LORD Jesus Christ, to become the Savior of the world. And, you'll realize, as never before, what the Bible means when it says that through Him, THE BLESSING has been given to us."[55]

Just as James 3:6 KJV tells us that the tongue can set on fire the course of nature, so can the blessing clear pathways and unlock the road to destiny when it is spoken. Every time there is a blessing in the Bible, it is spoken. There is power in the spoken word. Blessings must be spoken for power is in the tongue.

The Father's blessing is not set in stone, but it does pave the way and gives a child spiritual inclination to go to the father for instruction and direction. There is no evidence that there is any substance in it because the Father's blessing is spoken in faith and received in faith.

When we meet Abram, we do not know much of his past other than his genealogy and the location of where his father and his people had settled and were living. We know that he was from Ur and had been living in Haran. These were cities filled to the brim with wickedness. Nothing godly or anyone upright stood in those places. In this state, God looked on Abram with love and called him out of this mess and before Abram could obey or prove himself, God blessed him. Just as God showed his goodness and overwhelming love to his creation, Adam and Eve, by speaking His blessing over them just after He created them and before they were sent out into the world, God did the same for Abram.

Abram had settled in Haran. In this place devoid of hunger for God is where we find Abram. He had done nothing for God and had no accolades of which to boast. His life was headed nowhere great. Any indication would point to more of the same in regard to the path he was on in life. Yet, God singled him out right where he was and lovingly spoke His blessing over Abram.

"Now Yahweh said to Abram: 'Leave *it all behind* – your native land, your people, your father's household, and go to the land that I will show you. *Follow me*, and I will make you into a great nation. I will exceedingly bless and prosper you, and I will make you famous, so that you will be a *tremendous source of* blessing for others. I will bless all who bless you and curse all who curse you. And through you all the families of the earth will be blessed." (Genesis 12:1-3 TPT) We know that God encountered Abram on ten occasions and spoke more blessings over him. However, these future blessings are all related to and give more detail about this one.

Abram had a divine encounter with Yahweh, his Father. God spoke the blessing over Abram and this prophetic spoken blessing from the Father's heart changed the course of Abram's life, purpose, and destiny. It not only changed Abram's life, it changed Sarai's, it changed his descendants' lives, and it, through Jesus, has changed our lives as believers as well.

Everything God does is connected and designed perfectly and with intriguing order. It is fascinating that in the Hebrew language, the word for *thing* and *word* are the same. It is the Hebrew word *millah*.[56] In the design of God, *word* is the *thing*. When God speaks (and when we speak) His Word becomes the very thing that was spoken. "In the beginning was the Word, and the Word was with God, and the Word was God. He was in the beginning with God. All things were made through Him [The Word], and without Him nothing was made that was made....And the Word became flesh and dwelt among us, and we beheld His glory, the glory as of the only begotten of the Father, full of grace and truth." (John 1:1-3, 14

NKJV) God's Word contains the creative energy of God Himself.

God has such a high regard for the WORD that He has magnified His WORD above His Name (Psalms 138:2 KJV). God, in His sovereignty, has chosen to put Himself under the authority of His own WORD. Let that sink in for a moment. We know that He has the Name that is above every other name and that every knee will bow to His Name. Yet, even above His Name stands His WORD!

Knowing this, it only follows that it is impossible to have faith in anyone (God included) without knowing what they've said. We can have faith in what God says because Hebrews 6:18 KJV tells us plainly that it is impossible for God to lie. When God speaks, His Word is True and it will not ever be untrue.

The spoken blessing from God is true. What God speaks comes into existence. Jeremiah 1:12 KJV gives us further detail about God's word. It says, "Then said the Lord unto me, Thou hast well seen: for I will hasten my word to perform it." This is in alignment with what we already know about God's word. The word hasten means "to bring about speedily and to accelerate." This means that not only will God's word be true for all time, but that He will also work to make the *word* become the *thing* speedily.

Believing that God will hasten to bring His word to its fulfillment does not mean that God will do it in our human concept of what speedily means. We know that God spoke his Father's blessing over Abram when he was 75 years of age. We finally see the birth of the promised son, Isaac, when Abraham (his name had been changed by God) was 100 years old. This was a 25 year process. But, God's word was True when Abram was 75 and it was still true when he was 100.

Even though the process of seeing God's blessing come to pass over Abram initially took 25 years, in God's eyes, He did hasten His word. There was no way in the natural that Isaac could have been born to parents who were 90 and 100 years of age. God hastened and quickened (brought life) to Abraham and Sarah's bodies and the word God spoke became the essence of what was encoded in the word. Isaac was conceived and born. Isaac is just the beginning of the blessing coming to pass. God's blessing continues to this day.

Once God spoke the blessing over Abram, it started to work. Even when the natural eyes could not see the word working, it was working. Romans 8:28 KJV expounds, "And we know that all things work together for good to them that love God, to them who are the called according to his purpose". The word started working and everything began working together for Abram's good. Abram was called and the blessing could not help but take Abram on his journey to fulfill his purpose.

God takes us from "faith to faith" and from "glory to glory." He develops us in steps, a little at a time. (Romans 1:17 and 2 Corinthians 3:18 KJV) The spoken word and the spoken blessing of a father begins to activate when it is initially spoken. That doesn't mean it immediately comes to completion in the natural. We can see this in Abram's life where Isaac was born 25 years after the spoken blessing over Abram. However, as we have seen and discussed in various places in this book, God spoke and encountered Abram ten times over the course of that 25 plus year period. Each time, the intimacy of the encounter and the continued spoken blessing over him took Abram from where he was to where the blessing was taking him. Eventually, Abram became Abraham and the father of Isaac, the father of the Jewish people, and the Patriarch of our faith!

God took Abram a step at a time. Abram had to develop as a person. He had to grow in intimacy with God. He had to grow in faith in God and in his spoken word. After this time of development or hastening, the *word* became the *thing*! And the *word* is still to this day becoming the *thing*!

Ephesians 5:1 KJV instructs us to be followers or imitators of God, as little children. We are to follow God as His children. He is our Father and he is a good and loving Father. Even Jesus, being fully human and fully God, only followed this principle. "So Jesus said, 'I speak to you timeless truth. The Son is not able to do anything from himself or through my own initiative. I only do the works that I see the Father doing, for the Son does the same works as his Father." (John 5:19 TPT)

Jesus goes on to say several chapters later, "For I'm not speaking as someone who is self-appointed, but I speak by the authority of the Father himself who sent me, and who instructed me what to say... I speak the very words I've heard him speak" (John 12:49-50 TPT). Jesus only did what His Father did and said what His Father said. We would be wise to follow Jesus' example and be an imitator of our Father.

Imitating God can be done. We need a relationship with God as our Father, just as we have with our earthly father. The key is having a relationship. With this relationship, there is communication, speaking and listening on both sides, spending time together, and sharing your heart and letting God share His heart. In speaking the Father's blessing over children He loves, it is important to know that blessing is coming from absolute love. It is also important to know what falls in alignment with blessing and what falls in the opposite category of cursing. As easy as you may think it may be to figure out what falls in each category, some may be wondering about this.

To clarify what is a blessing and what is a curse, let's look at Deuteronomy

28. Here we find the first 14 verses expounding on what is a blessing and the rest of the verses in Chapter 28 detail what falls in the category of curse. I am going to include the verses 1-14 below. I really want to emphasize the difference between blessing and

cursing. When we imitate our Father, we look to the blessing and speak these over our children. If we are speaking anything that is in verses 15-68, we are speaking curses over our children. Therefore, we should only say what our Father says and speak blessing over our children.

> **Deuteronomy 28: 1-14 AMP –**
>
> Now it shall be, if you diligently listen to *and* obey the voice of the Lord your God, being careful to do all His commandments which I am commanding you today, the Lord your God will set you high above all the nations of the earth. All these blessings will come upon you and overtake you if you pay attention to the voice of the Lord your God. You *will be* blessed in the city, and you *will be* blessed in the field. The offspring of your body and the produce of your ground and the offspring of your animals, the offspring of your herd and the young of your flock *will be* blessed. Your basket and your kneading bowl *will be* blessed. You *will be* blessed when you come in and you *will be* blessed when you go out. The Lord will cause the enemies who rise up against you to be defeated before you; they will come out against you one way, but flee before you seven ways. The Lord will command the blessing upon you in your storehouses and in all that you undertake, and He will bless you in the land which the Lord your God gives you. The Lord will establish you as a people holy [and set apart] to Himself, just as He has sworn to you, if you keep the commandments of the Lord your God and walk [that is, live your life each and every day] in His ways. So all the peoples of the earth will see that you are called by the name of the Lord, and they will be afraid of you. The Lord will give you great prosperity, in the offspring of your body and in the offspring of your livestock and the produce of your ground, in the land which the Lord

> swore to your fathers to give you. The Lord will open for you His good treasure house, the heavens, to give rain to your land in its season and to bless all the work of your hand; and you will lend to many nations, but you will not borrow. The Lord will make you the head (leader) and not the tail (follower); and you will be above only, and you will not be beneath, if you listen *and* pay attention to the commandments of the Lord your God, which I am commanding you today, to observe them carefully. Do not turn aside from any of the words which I am commanding you today, to the right or to the left, to follow and serve other gods.

It is overwhelming to even comprehend all the fulness of the blessing in these verses above. In verse 2 it says that "all these blessings shall come upon you and overtake you if you heed the voice of the Lord your God". God has spoken the blessing over us. His spoken word has, from the moment it was spoken, immediately began to activate and hasten its performance. The blessing is hastening and coming on us and overtaking us. They are chasing us down!

God does not intend for us to struggle to receive these blessings. The very nature of the spoken word in the form of blessing means that the very way God intended and ordered the word to work will happen without our work or effort added to it. The word works on its own. It is not by our own effort or toil. This is the beauty of the loving nature of our Father. The blessing is just that – a blessing. It is not a reward. It is not a payment for our efforts. It is not even a trophy prize. It is a blessing just because of our identity as His children. Once the blessing is spoken, there is absolute certainty that God's word over our lives will happen.

Take a look at the verses in Deuteronomy 28:15 through 68. Just as wonderful as the blessing is, the curse is on the opposite extreme just as terrible. We must be diligent to watch our words that are spoken, for they really are spirit and life if we speak blessing. However, we have the choice of what words come out of our mouth. We make the choice of those words, and those words are a result of what is really alive in our hearts. Luke 6:45 AMP explains why this is so. "The upright (honorable, intrinsically good) man out of the good treasure [stored] in his heart produces what is upright (honorable and intrinsically good), and the evil man out of the evil storehouse brings forth that which is depraved (wicked and intrinsically evil); for out of the abundance (overflow) of the heart his mouth speaks."

Abraham knew the power of the blessing of his Father. He experienced the intimacy and the love that backed all of God's spoken blessing over him. Abraham saw firsthand in his life how God spoke the blessing over his life when he was at a place in his life where there was nothing apparently heading in a good direction. Abram was living in Haran and was 75 years old. He was already an old man. He had lived a long time with nothing really to show for it. He blended into the culture and society of his surroundings. Without His Father's blessing, he would have lived out his days doing more of the same thing and died. We would never have known that he ever existed, not knowing his name or anything about his life. However, all this changed for him with the blessing.

Abram went from a life devoid of blessing to a life full of blessing. From living in the curse to living in the blessing was a contrast for Abram. He went from a life of faith in what he had seen to the Father of our Faith in God. He went from childless to a father of nations. He went from a nobody to being famous. He went from being Abram to being Abraham. The activated spoken blessing was such a powerful and life transforming event for Abram that he imitated His Father and continued this tradition for his son, Isaac.

"Now, Yahweh had wonderfully blessed Abraham in every way, and he became a very old man, well advanced in years. One day,

Abraham *called for* his *trusted* head servant who oversaw all that he had, and said 'Please, put your hand here under my thigh, and I will make you swear by Yahweh, the God of heaven and earth, that you will not acquire a wife for my son among the Canaanites among whom I am living. Promise me you will go instead to my relatives in my native land and find a wife among them for my son Isaac.'" (Genesis 24:1-4 TPT) Abraham wanted to bless his son Isaac with a good wife and one that would bless Isaac. Abraham understood that the wife of Isaac would be a great influence over the children of Isaac, Abraham's grandchildren.

Rebekah, who became Isaac's wife, was just that. She was a blessing to Isaac and not only became the mother of twin boys, Jacob and Esau, but Isaac fell in love with Rebekah. This is important because it is the second time that love is mentioned between people in the Bible. The first time is Abraham's love for Isaac. This is the love of a father for his son. However, here, we find the first mention of a husband's love for his wife. This is significant and I believe is a huge blessing that Abraham wanted for his son. Isaac not only had a beautiful wife and a good wife, but he loved her. Love is a blessing.[57]

Just as God had blessed Abram, God also blessed Isaac. "After Abraham had passed, God greatly blessed his son Isaac, and Isaac settled near the well named the Well of the Living One Who Watches Over Me." (Genesis 25:11 TPT) This is the same well as where Hagar once cried out to God for help and mercy and God heard her. Also, Ishmael drank from this well of grace. Isaac did not just visit this well, this place where God sees our problems and hears us. Isaac dwelled there. He made it his settlement, his habitation, and by doing that he made His Father, the all-seeing God his source of supply – the blessing.[58]

Isaac also blessed Jacob and continued the tradition of the father's blessing to his son. We know the story of how Jacob was the younger twin and Esau was the oldest. Esau, in fact had the blessing of the birthright because he was the oldest and he would be in line for his father's blessing because of his firstborn status. However, Jacob, even from birth was grabbing on his brother's heel trying to get in line and be the firstborn. Jacob's name means supplanter or deceiver or one who replaces another.

Jacob followed through with just that. He wanted to replace Esau with himself and in effect, receive all the benefits and blessings that would otherwise be Esau's. Esau did not value his birthright very much, because he sold and surrendered it to Jacob for one bowl of lentils. Esau was very hungry and being so dramatic said, "What good is the birthright if I'm dead" (Genesis 25:27-34 TPT)?

Much later, when Isaac was dying and ready to speak his blessing over each son, Jacob again was able to gain what was meant for Esau. He, with the help and idea of his mother, dressed as Esau and went to his father with fresh game he had prepared as a meal. Isaac's vision was not very good and he had to rely on touch and smell. Jacob had done a good job of convincing Isaac that he was Esau and with that, Isaac spoke his father's blessing over Jacob:

"Ah, the smell of my son is like the smell of a lush field that Yahweh has blessed! May God give you heaven's dew, the fatness of earth, and an abundance of grain and new wine! Let peoples serve you and nations bow down to you! May you be master over your brothers and may your mother's sons bow down to you! Those who curse you will be cursed and those who bless you will be blessed!" (Genesis 27:27-29 TPT)

In Genesis chapters 48 and 49, Jacob speaks blessings over his children and grandchildren. "Let me prophesy to you about your future *destinies*." (Genesis 49:1 TPT) "Jacob became a shaper of destiny for his children as God revealed to him the future of his sons. His prophecies were based both on their character and on their actions.

He spoke into their destinies and described God's plan for each one. Genesis 49 also prophesies to the day in which we live. The rest of the Old Testament and all the New Testament are the development of Genesis 49. These verses require the whole Bible for their understanding. How profound are the prophecies of Jacob!"⁵⁹

The blessing that Jacob spoke over Judah is noteworthy as we look and examine the Father's blessing and its lineage from God to us today! "O Judah, your brothers will praise you. You will conquer your foes in battle, and your father's sons will bow down before you. Judah, you are like a young lion who has devoured its prey, my son, and departed. Like a lion, he crouches and lies down, and like a lioness – who dares to awaken him? The scepter of rulership will not be taken from Judah, nor the ruler's staff from his descendants, until the Shiloh comes and takes what is due him, for the obedience of nations belongs to him. He will tether his donkey to the vine and his purebred cold to the choicest branch. He will wash his garments in wine and his robe in the blood of grapes. His eyes are more exhilarating than wine and his teeth whiter than milk." (Genesis 49:8-12 TPT)

The blessing over Judah is profound because it points to Jesus, the coming Messiah, a descendant of Judah. "Judah is a wonderful picture of the One who is seen as the Mighty Lion of Judah. For Jesus Christ is the One who places his omnipotent hand on the neck of his enemies and delivers us. The lion, the king of beasts, terrifies its prey with his roar. When he seizes his prey, no one can resist him. After he has seized his prey, no one pursues him or seeks revenge, for the lion is a conqueror. Judah is compared to three kinds of lions: a young lion, a mature hunting lion, and a lioness. This is more than a prophecy of the tribe of Judah becoming strong and mighty; it is a prophecy of One who will come from Judah to devour his prey Jesus is not a raging Lion; he is a resting Lion who has conquered every foe. He crouched and took his cross, but ow lies down in perfect peace. His victory is total and secure. Who would dare rouse a lion when he is lying down after his kill, and who would rouse a lioness while she is guarding her cubs? These three phrases to describe the lion are truly descriptive of what our Savior-King has done for us! Jesus came as our Savior, 'a young lion.' He laid down his life on the cross to destroy the one who held us in fear of death. He was raised again to be seated at God's right hand, 'like a lion, he crouches and lies down.' Today, he guards us with tender love and compassion, 'like a lioness.'"[60]

Everything about the blessing from the very beginning points us to Jesus! Jesus became THE SEED of Abraham. From the blessing in the Garden to Adam and Eve... to the blessing of Abraham...to the blessing of Isaac and Jacob...to the blessing of Judah prophesying the coming, purpose and destiny of Jesus, the Father's blessing was not only for our patriarchs, but for us today.

Jesus did not come as the seed of Abraham so He could receive the blessing. He came so that we could receive that very blessing. In fact, "Jesus, our Messiah, was cursed in our place and in so doing, dissolved the curse from our lives, so that all the blessings of Abraham can be poured out upon even non-Jewish believers" (Galatians 3:14 TPT).

The curse which came in the earth as a result of the fall of man in the Garden of Eden has been working just as the blessing works. Both are working. However, we don't have to live under the curse. Jesus, THE SEED of Abraham, took on everything under the curse and He was cursed in our place so we don't have to live that way. Because of Jesus' victory in defeating EVERYTHING under the curse, we can live in THE BLESSING. This is how God intended us to live from the very beginning. Before He sent Adam and Eve into their purpose and destiny, He blessed them. That blessing is reserved for us today!

We don't have to live our lives struggling with sickness and pain, with not enough money to pay our bills, or with anxiety and fear. If you read clearly what is outlined in Deuteronomy 28 from verse 15 until the end of that chapter, these are all part of the curse. Some Christians even believe and teach that this is all just normal and how life is, and we should just be patient and work to get through these. But Jesus came so that we would have authority over ALL those curses. We don't have to accept that kind of life as normal. Jesus came to free us from that life. He has come to take us from that place of cursing to a place of blessing. The exciting thing is that "since you've been united to Jesus the Messiah, you are now Abraham's 'child' and inherit all the promises of the kingdom realm" (Galatians 3:29 TPT)!

The Father's blessing is not about where you've been but where you are going. The Father looks beyond where you are today and sees into your potential. Some people don't believe they are worthy to receive the Father's blessing. The critical component of the blessing is that it is not based on your worthiness. It is only based on your status as His child. You have great value to your Father. This is why He has spoken great blessings over you and wants to speak more over you. Just because He loves us, He looks beyond where we are today. He wants to communicate His love to us. He really just wants us to know Him in his fullness.

In the chaos swirling in the world today, don't overlook the importance and significance of the Father's blessing. First and foremost, looking to God as Father and receiving His perfect and loving blessing over your life. With the Father drawing close to us, it allows us to draw close to others and bless our own children or others that are like "children" to us. Secondly, take time to speak blessing over your children. Even if you are not a father, but are a mother, or a friend, or an aunt or uncle, take time to speak into your "children" and prophesy blessings over them. Thirdly, if you have never received a blessing from your earthly father, take time to reconcile that issue.

So many want a father's blessing, but some feel they have lost out on. Let hope drive you to ask for and receive a father's blessing. There are many different scenarios regarding relationships with fathers. Some have fathers who didn't know they could bless their children, some have fathers who unfortunately were just bad, and some may have passed prematurely.

Even if your father isn't bad but never blessed you, he can still give you a blessing. Go to your father and ask him to bless you. He may give you a variety of responses. He may say he doesn't know how or doesn't know why it is important. He may be hesitant or awkward. But he will want to do it because he wants you to be successful and feel loved.

It's not too late. Even if you are a father and haven't received one, you can give one.

A heart that is hardened to the earthly father is one that will be difficult to receive the Heavenly father. Forgiveness is a spiritual event, yet we feel it in our soul. Forgiveness is spiritual atmosphere you need to live in. Forgiveness is a paving machine for the road to blessing.

Jesus is the ultimate example of forgiveness. Our sin caused his death, and he forgave us for it. This is the reality and truth of forgiveness. Forgiveness allows our heavenly Father to make up the difference between what the earthly father could not fill. He fills the void between what should have been done and what was done - Only our Father can fill this gap!

John Paul Jackson once spoke a Father's Blessing from himself as an earthly father and man to those within the sound of his voice. He began with the blessing as seen in Numbers 6 when God blessed the children of Israel under the pronouncement of Moses.

Upon blessing the people, God would place His name and bless those who heard it. That means you.

As you read the blessing below, say it out loud as a blessing over yourself. You can also give it to your father to speak over you. John Paul Jackson spoke it in faith. Now, you receive the blessing in faith:

"May the Lord bless you and keep you, the Lord make His face shine upon you and be gracious to you. The Lord lift up His countenance upon you and give you peace.

And from me, from my heart, as a father and a grandfather, I'd like to bless you in this way…

May you reach the purpose for which you were created. May you have courage above your peers. May you have more passion for the things of God as others think is necessary. May you dream more than others think is practical. May you expect more than others think is possible. May you choose wisely without earthly bias. You have people to influence that you've not yet met. You have lives to change that are awaiting for your arrival. You are strategically placed wherever God takes you by His grand design just so you can become everything He made you to be. That place is the place you can grow best. That place is the place where you can be most fruitful, the place where the futures change because of your presence. May you see vistas that others don't even know exist. May you see God in every petal of every flower and every blade of grass for each of them are designed by His hand. May you bless your children and may they become giants under the faith under the mighty hand of God. You won't fail. You were made by God to be here for such a time as this."[61]

CHAPTER 11

Hall of Famer – The Father of Our Faith

Abraham is a remarkable man. He stands out from the crowd and was set apart from the wickedly noisy hustle of Haran and Ur ever since we meet him in Genesis chapter 11. There is something profound about his journey that we are drawn to. Abraham is known as the Father of Faith, and for obvious reasons. We look to him to learn from his successes and shortcomings, and all the while gleaning from his journey, we must remember that Abraham was just as much human and you and me. There was nothing inherently special or superhuman about him. He was just a man. Yet, he allowed faith in God to take him on a remarkable journey to receiving the promise.

There is a very popular song written by and made famous by the Irish pop rock band *The Script* called "Hall of Fame." The bridge of the song refers to people of all kinds, ages, and professions who will be on the walls of the Hall of Fame.

Be students, be teachers

Be politicians, be preachers Yeah

Be believers, be leaders

Be astronauts, be champions

Be truth-seekers

Be students, be teachers

Be politicians, be preachers Yeah

Be believers, be leaders

Be astronauts, be champions

The lyrics of this song explain that it doesn't matter who you are or where you are from or anything about you for you to be successful. You can rise to be in the Hall of Fame for being an overcomer and achieving success in whatever you do. The world has its version of success and how that is achieved. But we know that real success ultimately will only come from the guidance and wisdom found in a relationship with Yahweh! Abraham certainly had that relationship with God and through his numerous personal encounters with God, received instruction, guidance, and encouragement from Yahweh Himself.

Hebrews chapter 11 is known as the Faith Hall of Fame. In this chapter, we learn some very important truths about faith, what faith is, and how it works. We also get to look at all the people who are on the walls of the Faith Hall of Fame. From Abel, Enoch, and Noah to Abraham and Sarah, to others who are unnamed who endured atrocities for their faith. There is something very remarkable about each of these people and they stand out regarding their faith for very good reason. Abraham is no exception.

In Hebrews chapter 11, there is more written about Abraham than all the other Hall of Famers. Out of 40 verses, Abraham is written about in 11 of those verses. He takes up almost 28% of chapter 11. That only leaves 72% for all the other Hall of Famers combined as well as insight into faith itself. That is remarkable because the others who were commended for their faith stand out from the crowd in their own merit. However, Abraham rises to the top of the crowd in this elite group. He is not just a Faith Hall of Famer. He is known as the Father of our Faith. He is the cream of the cream!

Merriam Webster dictionary defines a Hall of Fame as "a structure housing memorials to famous or illustrious individuals usually chosen by a group of electors or a group of individuals in a particular category (such as a sport) who have been selected as particularly illustrious".⁶² These individuals who are selected to be in a Hall of Fame are noteworthy for their achievements in their respective field. They are well respected and honored for their contribution and level of achievement.

A significant aspect of becoming a member of a Hall of Fame is that the person does not nominate or vote for himself to be inducted. Other people nominate and there is a committee within each Hall of Fame organization that thoroughly examines the character and professional achievement of that individual. For example, to be inducted into the Pro Football Hall of Fame, "every candidate is carefully scrutinized and must receive at least 80 percent approval of the Selection Committee at the annual meeting before he can be selected…When the Selectors meet in February on the eve of the Super Bowl in this host city to name the newest class members, they will have before them a roster of 18 finalists, along with detailed biographies on each".⁶³

Similarly, there is a rigorous selection process to be inducted into the Country Music Hall of Fame. To be elected into this prestigious group is the highest honor that a country music performer, writer, or professional can receive. This is a very exclusive group to join. Unlike the Pro Football Hall of Fame which inducts 18 new individuals each year, the Country Music Hall of Fame only inducts 3 new members each year. There is a category for each three: "Modern Era" which are individuals eligible for induction 20 years after they achieve national prominence; "Veteran's Era" which means eligible after 45 years after they achieve national prominence; "Non-Performer, Songwriter, and Recording and/or Touring Musician active prior to 1980".

The Country Music Hall of Fame does not publish their official rules and hasn't for over 50 years now, so the exclusivity of this group is coveted even more by those in the country music industry. They have one interesting known rule which is that if someone has passed away, they cannot be voted on until one year has passed since their death to decrease sympathy votes.⁶⁴

Just like these football players who have achieved exceptional records in their career and extremely talented musicians who are recognized for their outstanding success, we have individuals who have displayed a rare achievement in the exercise of their faith. Hebrews chapter 11 is where we see all the individuals who have been inducted into this exclusive group. They have achieved one of the highest honors by being commended for their faith. They are to be celebrated, admired, and if we are wise, we should learn a thing or two from their journey.

The author of Hebrews is unknown, but could possibly be Paul, and writes what we know as the book of Hebrews. However, this writing is more of a sermon contained in the form of this letter. At the time this was written, some significant events were happening. There were Jewish people who had converted from Judaism to Christianity. Living out this conversion was proving to be challenging because the government and society were unleashing hurt on those new Christians. It is thought that during this time, Emperor Nero was in power. This new religion had been outlawed.

Emperor Nero blamed the new Christians for setting fire to Rome in AD

64. In addition, the Jews who still practiced traditional Judaism persecuted those who had converted to Christianity. This had been going on for more than 30 years. The Jewish Christians were growing tired of this life and the difficulties and persecution Christianity had brought on them. Not surprisingly, they were tempted, and some did revert to their old religion of Judaism. They stopped meeting with fellow Christians and began to go back to their old synagogues.⁶⁵

We can identify with those Christians as the current political, religious, and social climate of today is anti-Christian and we see a spirit of anti-Christ running with determined energy in the world. We are seeing a tremendous push for silencing of Christians and double standards for what applies to churches and Christian meeting places as opposed to gatherings in other places. We see in other parts of the world where extremist groups are torturing and killing Christians just because they profess Christ as their Lord. We can see how much more comfortable it would be to assimilate with those not being silenced or persecuted.

However, the writer of Hebrews has a mission of encouraging these new Christians and giving them ammunition for the fight of staying with their new faith. "Along the way, the author teaches them – and us – about the superiority of Christ above the religious institutions of Moses and the Old Testament. The sermon-letter is filled with references to the old sacrificial system and priesthood of ancient Israel and explains how Jesus' death has replaced this old religious system – making it the perfect book to understand how Jesus' story fulfills Israel's history!... He is our magnificent High Priest who is greater than Moses, greater than any sacrifice ever offered, greater than any prophet of old. He perfects our faith…"[66]

As we get well into Hebrews, we find the writer gives the readers a call to persevere. The writer encourages Christians to stay the course and not be tempted to fall back to old ways and old mindsets. Even though you may be mistreated and persecuted for your faith, publicly and shamefully treated, "don't lose your bold, courageous faith, for you are destined for a great reward" (Hebrews 10:35 TPT)! We are not the held back ones, but are the ones who experience true life. We live from the very faith of Christ. It is not even our own faith to begin with, but it is a gift from Jesus Himself when we make Him the Lord of our life. Jesus is completely victorious, and He gifts to us His faith so that we can live from that very faith. (Hebrews 10:38 TPT)

With this exhortation and great affirmation, the author of Hebrews leads the reader into the Faith Hall of Fame and proudly walks us through its walls filled with brothers and sisters of our faith which have persevered and clung to the promise. Every one of these people who have been inducted into this great Hall of Fame overcame and held tightly to the promise of God for their lives. Every single one of these people are simply human as you and I, but they allowed faith to take them higher and higher. They overcame and succeeded when reality screamed that it was completely impossible. This is the power of bold faith.

"Now faith brings our hopes into reality and becomes the foundation needed to acquire the things we long for. It is all the evidence required to prove what is still unseen." (Hebrews 11:1 TPT) This is faith. Faith reaches out into the future and draws hope into the present. Hope is for the future, but faith is for right now. We always need hope for the things of the future. However, if hope stays as hope, it is always somewhere in the future, never bringing the promise into the present reality. We know that hope deferred makes the heart sick. "When hope's dream seems to drag on and on, the delay can be depressing. But when at last your dream comes true, life's sweetness will satisfy your soul." (Proverbs 13:12 TPT) So, we must use faith, as a fishing rod, to reel in the catch. We can see a great fish out in the water and always hope for it, but we need to get the rod of faith and bring it in. We need to catch the fish and reel in the promise.

Abraham is the shining example in the Faith Hall of Fame. It is for a very good reason that he is called the Father of our Faith. We have studied the life of Abraham in a lot of detail in this book. We know his journey well as we have traveled in his sandals of faith. Let's discover what Hebrews 11 highlights in terms of why he is included as a Faith Hall of Famer. I think it is appropriate to read through from beginning to end the faith accolades of Abraham:

Abraham's Accolades in the Faith Hall of Fame

"Faith motivated Abraham to obey God's call and leave the familiar to discover the territory he was destined to inherit from God. So he left with only a promise and without even knowing ahead of time where he was going. Abraham stepped out in faith. He lived by faith as an immigrant in his promised land as though it belonged to someone else. He journeyed through the land living in tents with Isaac and Jacob who were persuaded that they were also co-heirs of the same promise.

His eyes of faith were set on the city with unshakable foundations, whose architect and builder is God himself. Sarah's faith embraced the miracle power to conceive even though she was barren and was past the age of childbearing, for the authority of her faith rested in the One who made the promise, and she tapped into his faithfulness.

In fact, so many children were subsequently fathered by this aged man of faith—one who was as good as dead, that he now has offspring as innumerable as the sand on the seashore and as the stars in the sky!

These heroes all died still clinging to their faith, not even receiving all that had been promised them. But they saw beyond the horizon the fulfillment of their promises and gladly embraced it from afar. They all lived their lives on earth as those who belonged to another realm.

For clearly, those who live this way are longing for the appearing of a heavenly city. And if their hearts were still remembering what they left behind; they would have found an opportunity to go back.

But they couldn't turn back for their hearts were fixed on what was far greater, that is, the heavenly realm!

So because of this God is not ashamed in any way to be called their God, for he has prepared a heavenly city for them.

Faith operated powerfully in Abraham for when he was put to the test he offered up Isaac. Even though he received God's promises of descendants, he was willing to offer up his only son! For God had promised,

"Through your son Isaac your lineage will carry on your name."

Abraham's faith made it logical to him that God could raise Isaac from the dead, and symbolically, that's exactly what happened." (Hebrews 11:8-19 TPT)

Now that we have read what the writer of Hebrews is emphasizing to be Abraham's faith credentials, successes, and outstanding achievements, let's examine and draw out the gold nuggets! The very first introduction in the Faith Hall of Fame tells us that it is highly commendable in the faith arena that faith motivated Abraham to obey God's call and leave what was familiar to him and go to where God instructed him. Abraham obeyed God and boldly stepped out in faith to go to a foreign land where he was an immigrant. Back in Genesis chapter 12, when God encountered Abram for the first time, God instructed Abram to "Leave it all behind". (Genesis 12:1 TPT). From this very first encounter with Yahweh, Abram shines as a faith warrior. His first and immediate response to Yahweh's instructions is to obey. "So, Abram obeyed Yahweh and left." (Genesis 12:4 TPT)

Faith motivated Abram to obey! This simple yet extremely powerful act of obeying has elevated Abram onto the stage for all the world to see. Abram, a very ordinary man, living in a city overflowing with wickedness all around him, having no measured achievements to speak of, just simply obeyed when he heard God speak. Something inside Abram's spirit knew that this Yahweh was who He said He was, and Abram did not doubt, but obeyed. He knew the unmistakable voice of His Maker!!!

<u>Abram obeyed immediately.</u> We see this immediate compliance over and over in Abram's journey as Yahweh encounters him and instructs and speaks blessing over him. The saying, "obedience delayed is disobedience" is very true. When God speaks and instructs us, He expects to obey immediately. Otherwise, we are acting in disobedience. I have used this phrase in teaching my children the importance of obeying immediately and not when you feel like it. Also, "partial obedience is disobedience." It is very important that we immediately and completely obey the instructions from Yahweh.

Abram did not need to know where he was going, only that God had instructed him to go. So often, we hesitate to obey because we aren't sure where we are going or how we will get there. If we believe that God has already caused us to reach that destination and has made a way for us, then our faith is in Yahweh and His word. Otherwise, we would be putting faith in ourselves and that is a heavy load to carry. In fact, that load is so heavy, we would be crushed. The load gets even lighter when we remember that it is not even our own faith in Yahweh, but we live from the faith that has been gifted to us from Christ Himself, a faith that is so perfect and unblemished, and completely victorious. (Hebrews 10:38 TPT).

<u>Abram stepped out in faith.</u> Obeying required Abram to do something. He had to initially take one step. From where Abram was to get to where Yahweh intended for his destiny, Abram had to act. He had to respond to what God said. Obedience does not just mean that we say "Yes"! and that ends our part. Yahweh gave us a free will to act. He is not going to do the obedience for us. Abram

had to willingly move his own feet forward. God's part does not include lifting our feet and putting them down to miraculously take steps he instructs us to take.

<u>Abram lived by faith.</u> He lived as an immigrant in his promised land as if it belonged to someone else. He journeyed and traveled through this land and lived in tents. He lived as a nomad and a wanderer, with no settled place established to call "home." He continued to live this way even when Isaac was born. Even though he had received the promise of his son, Isaac, Abraham still had to continue living in the land God promised him as his very own as an immigrant would. He taught his son and this lesson of living by faith was passed on to successive generations so that Isaac and Jacob were persuaded that they were co-heirs of the same promise.

<u>Abram had eyes of faith.</u> Abram set his sights and positioned his focus on the eternal city whose architect and builder is God. He was continually receiving this city designed by God with unshakable foundations. In Hebrews 11:1 TPT, we know that faith is explained as "the foundation needed to acquire the things we long for". Abram used faith for his vision instead of his natural eyes. Faith could see the unseen and was the foundation for him to acquire the city he longed for. In the face of reality, Abram dismissed what could be seen and perceived by his natural senses in lieu of a clearer perspective that was more real than his natural reality.

<u>Sarah's faith embraced God's miracle power.</u> Abram's faith flowed over into his wife, Sarai. We find that not only did Abram achieve great exploits of faith, but Sarai did also. I believe that she was inspired and encouraged by Abram's tight embracing grip on faith. Even when Sarah was 90 years old, she embraced God's miracle power to conceive the promised son even though she had been barren her entire life. Sarah had a dead womb and at an age when she should never be able to conceive, she defied death in multiple ways to produce life.

Sarah's faith rested in the authority of the One who made the promise. Yahweh made the promise that Sarah would conceive and be the mother of the promised son, Isaac. It is the authority of Yahweh that we see here being supreme. God authorized the promise, and He authored the promise. It is His authority alone that is the rock in her slingshot of faith. Sarah's faith rests in Yahweh's authority, not in her own authority, or Abraham's authority. This passage says that Sarah's faith rested. Her faith did not toil or struggle to find some anchoring in Yahweh. It simply rested. Resting means that the subject we are speaking of does not work any longer toward a goal, but rather stops striving and begins to relax and refresh. By resting, we recover strength.

When we think of the benefits of resting our natural bodies, we understand that it gives the body a chance to recover from its work and during this time of rest, it rejuvenates. Resting also helps to boost our immune system. This is particularly important because our immune system is what our body uses as a line of defense against foreign invaders and helps to provide a barrier to sickness and disease that would attack the body. This is a parallel principle spiritually. When we allow our faith to rest in the authority of Yahweh, we are boosting our spiritual immune system. This is helping to strengthen it and keep out foreign invaders that would attack it like doubt and unbelief. Sarah tapped into the faithfulness of God and rested in His authority instead of working to help faith out. Faith works by resting in Yahweh's authority.

This is the importance of the Sabbath, or day of rest. God perfectly designed our bodies and created our bodies to require one day out of 7 to rest and recover. When we continue to plow through life with no periodic break or rest, we diminish significantly our capacity to be our best. As we see here, Sarah utilized this principle of Sabbath or rest to apply in its fullest form to the action of her faith. Her faith did something powerful – it rested.

<u>Abraham clung to his faith.</u> In the 25-year journey Abraham had from the initial promise spoken by Yahweh to the birth of Isaac, we see Abraham respond to God with immediate obedience. This two and a half decades were filled with periodic encounters with Yahweh and as Abraham approached his 99th birthday, he had no visible sign of any part of the promise coming to pass. However, Abraham did not let go of the words of God that were spoken directly to him. After 25 years, at the age of 100, finally, and miraculously, Isaac was born. This truly was a miracle of faith. The conception of Isaac and his birth by a mother who was 90 years old defied any logical expectation. However, the fact remains that Isaac was born to parents who were 90 and 100 years old.

There was more to the promise from Yahweh. Not only was there to be a promised son, but Abraham was also to be made into a great nation, Abraham was to be exceedingly blessed and prospered by God, Abraham was to become famous, and he was to be a tremendous source of blessing to others. God promised Abraham the land as far as he could see in every direction that it would belong to him and his descendants. Abraham was a very old man when Isaac was born. The reality is that Abraham saw only the beginning of the promise come to pass. The beginning was a miracle.

Abraham died still clinging to his faith. Having received only a portion of the promise, there a significant majority of the promise he never saw with his own eyes come to pass. However, he saw beyond the horizon the fulfillment and still embraced it from afar. He lived his life on earth as though he belonged to another realm. (Hebrews 11:13 TPT)

Abraham longed for more than the promise. He longed for the appearing of a heavenly city, or his eternal homeland. This is a country and a place which was prepared, designed, and built by Yahweh. This eternal homeland was to Abraham far more desirable than even the promise of the natural homeland Yahweh promised to him and his descendants forever.

The first instruction Yahweh gave to Abram is so key here. Yahweh said to Abram, "Leave it all behind" (Genesis 12:1 TPT). God could not fulfill his destiny for Abram if he kept remembering what he left behind. Abraham needed to leave it all behind and not turn his eyes back to the past but keep them on the promise. Abraham clung to his faith for the promise of God in the natural realm, but he also clung to the promise of God in the spiritual realm because he longed for the appearing of a heavenly city and did not look for an opportunity to go back. His heart was fixed on what was far greater which is the heavenly realm. This is why God is not ashamed to be called Abraham's God. When we refer to the Patriarchs (Abraham, Isaac, and Jacob), we refer to their God as the God of Abraham, Isaac, and Jacob. God is not ashamed to be their God because Abraham's (and the successive Patriarchs) hearts were fixed on the heavenly realm.

<u>Abraham's faith operated powerfully.</u> After Abraham went through all those years believing and trusting Yahweh for the promise to come to pass, Abraham was faced with the most important test of all. After a lifetime of waiting for his promised son, Isaac, he was finally born. Isaac was a real, living person born to Abraham and Sarah. I'm sure that every time Abraham looked at Isaac, he remembered his journey of faith to receive Isaac. But Yahweh tested Abraham with the test of a lifetime. Yahweh told Abraham to sacrifice Isaac. We know that Abraham set off immediately the very next morning on the journey to Mount Moriah and did not hesitate to obey. How could Yahweh ask Abraham to sacrifice THE PROMISE SON that he had waited for? How could it be possible that Isaac would be sacrificed? It would be through Isaac's lineage that the promise would carry on.

"Even though Abraham received God's promises of descendants, he was willing to offer up his only son!" (Hebrews 11:17 TPT) This is the key. Abraham was willing. Abraham still trusted God even with this seemingly contradictory request. In the face of killing the life he was promised, Abraham was willing to obey God. This brings us full circle to where we started in Abraham's faith achievements. Abraham started by obeying God and leaving it all behind. Now, we see Abraham obey God and his willingness to do whatever God asked. Abraham was obedient. This is what God saw in Abram from the very beginning.

<u>Abraham's faith made it logical.</u> Every instruction that God gave to Abraham was obeyed: From leaving his homeland to journey to an unknown place and living as an immigrant in that land, to this ultimate test of being willing to sacrifice his son, Isaac. Abraham had walked with God for so long and journeyed the road of faith believing and embracing every word from Yahweh. When faced with the test of sacrificing his promised son, Isaac, Abraham's faith made it logical to obey the instructions of God instead of reasoning that it was contradictory to God's promise. Abraham didn't know how that Isaac could be the one whose lineage carried on the promise, but Abraham knew that God could do the impossible. Abraham knew that no matter what, God would remain faithful and stay true to his word and his promise. He had seen God come through time after time.

So, "Abraham's faith made it logical to him that God could raise Isaac from the dead, and symbolically, that's exactly what happened" (Hebrews 11:19 TPT). The faith that Abraham had was so strong and so committed, that no matter how illogical it may have sounded to natural ears, God's instructions are always logical. Abraham's faith cut through anything that would seem illogical to make it logical. Abraham had a personal and intimate relationship with Yahweh. He knew that if God had promised something, His word was true no matter what. Abraham knew that the promise was already a settled matter and he was not going to question that.

And right on time, a ram showed up in the thicket just as Abraham's arm had been raised in the air with the ax. As Abraham looked down at his promise, with the arm of obedience in the air, a ram that God Himself provided showed up to be the sacrifice instead of Isaac. And so, symbolically, God did raise Isaac from the dead with the provision of the substitute sacrifice. Faith proved victorious in reeling in, keeping the promise, and pulling in the ability for the fullness of the promise to come to pass.

It is noteworthy here to point out that Abraham is commended for his faith in the Faith Hall of Fame. He is not commended on an outcome. It was the job of Abraham to have faith in God. It was God's responsibility to fulfill the promise he made to Abraham. Faith holds tight to the promise. It isn't the jurisdiction of faith to figure out how and why and when you can get to the promise or the destiny. God has already created the end from the beginning. He has that part already perfectly orchestrated. So, we call Hebrews chapter 11 the Faith Hall of Fame, not the Outcome Hall of Fame. The illustrious individuals who are commemorated in this Hall of Fame are there because of their exploits of faith only. They are not and we are not responsible for the outcome. We are responsible and our job is to have faith in God.

The word "faith" in Hebrew is *enumah*. In Hebrews chapter 11, we often hear that faith is the substance of things hoped for and the evidence of things not yet seen (Hebrews 11:1 KJV). In this definition of faith, we see it as a noun. It is a substance and it is evidence. I have heard faith called the currency of heaven. The Hebrew word means firmness, figuratively security, morally fidelity, stability, and truth.[67] Literally, enumah means "to take firm action". So, faith we have seen is a noun, but here we also find that it is a verb. Faith is an act. A good analogy to faith is a staircase. You may, on an intellectual level, know that the stairs lead up to the next level, but until you put one foot forward and go up, you will not actually experience the next level. You would not just believe that the stairs exist if you need to go to the next level, you would actually climb the stairs.[68]

A good example of what faith means is in Exodus 17:12 KJV, where "Moses' hands were heavy; and they took a stone, and put it under him, and he sat there on; and Aaron and Hur stayed up his hands, the one on the one side, and the other on the other side; and his hands were steady until the going down of the sun". In this verse, we see that enumah "is an action-oriented word meaning "support". This is important because the Western concept of faith places the action on the one you have faith in, such as 'faith in God'. But the Hebrew word אֱמוּנָה places the action on the one who "supports God." It is not a knowing that God will act, but rather "I will do what I can do to support God".[69] In the verse above, we see that it is the support or the enumah of Aaron and Hur that held up Moses' arms. It was not the support of Moses himself.

Moses had told Joshua to choose men to go and fight Amalek. He explained that the next day, he would stand on the top of the hill with the rod of God in his hands. When Moses held up his hands, the Israelites prevailed and when he lowered his hands, the Amalekites prevailed. But after so long, Moses' hands grew tired and heavy. So, the men took a stone and positioned it for Moses to sit on. Then Aaron and Hur held up his hands, one on each side of Moses. It was the support of Aaron and Hur that held up Moses' hands. This is the enumah or the support for Moses' hands staying in the air so that the Israelites would be victorious against the enemy. (Exodus 17:9-12 AMP)

Faith is the substance of things hoped for and the evidence of things yet unseen. It is also an action that supports that substance. Just as Aaron and Hur supported Moses' arms to stay high in the air tozzz ensure victory for the Israelites, we see the willing and faithful obedience of Abraham, the support or the enumah, which held up the promise of God in front of him. Faith is and faith does. We often hear that "Faith without works is dead." This comes from James 2:14 KJV. Another way to phrase that is, "What good is it if someone claims to have faith but demonstrates no good works to prove it?" (James 2:14 TPT). We can claim to have the substance, but if there is no action supporting that claim, the desire is as dead because it will never be brought into reality.

This action is a main emphasis in the accolades of Abraham in the Faith Hall of Fame. He was steadfast, he was consistent, but most importantly, he was obedient. The obedience of Abraham was his support (enumah) for holding up the promise of God. The faith that we see in Hebrews 11:1, being the substance or the currency of heaven, must be spent or exchanged for the promise and the destiny. This is done by acting on that exchange or an action-oriented step to support the exchange taking place. We need both, the substance and the support. Abraham had both.

In "Contemplations on Character", Brian Guerin references Rolland Buck's encounter with an angel: "The records in heaven keep no account of the wrongs of believers." Even though men may fail, in God's love, their fallenness is not recorded in heaven. "Even the account of failures of men in the Bible have been penned for our sake, yet they aren't recorded in heaven. Even in Hebrews we see the "hall of faith" (see Hebrews 11). In it, the Holy Spirit inspired the author to write about the various legends of the Bible, be it David, Abraham, Noah and more. Yet through this New Covenant lens, the writer does not bring out their shortcomings and failure– even though they had plenty. He emphasizes their great faith. God keeps no list by which he judges men. He judges us by Christ's blood."[70]

Abraham truly was an exceptional man. He went from darkness into light. He crossed over from doubt to faith. He is ranked number 1 in the Faith Hall of Fame which he deserves. He used faith to receive the promises of God. He is the Patriarch, the Father of Isaac and Jacob. His natural descendants are called the Jewish people, the Israelites, and became known as the Hebrews. This is so very fitting because the name Hebrews means "those who crossed over". Abraham fathered those who would cross over from shadow to substance. Every promise that God promised him has transpired. Even though Abraham died still clinging to the complete fulfillment of the promise, those promises have been coming to pass and are still coming to pass today. God did make Abraham into a great nation. God did exceedingly bless and prosper Abraham. God did make him famous so that he would be a tremendous source of blessing for others. God blesses all who bless Abraham (and his seed) and curses all who curses him. And through Abraham, all the families of the world are being blessed. Jesus Christ descended from Abraham and is the greatest blessing the world has ever and will ever have.

Abraham left it all behind. He willingly obeyed Yahweh. Abraham traveled far and long in his sandals of faith. Will you also exchange shoes of mediocrity and put on your own sandals of faith?

Crystal G.H. Lowery
P.O. Box 410
Isle of Palms, SC 29451

Website: www.basedonfaith.org

Email: info@basedonfaith.org

Your financial support of this non-profit 501(c)3 ministry is appreciated.

Order Crystal's Devotional Book

Sweet Love Letters to Jesus (English language)

https://www.amazon.com/Sweet-Love-Letters-Jesus-Devotional/dp/1684118557/ref=sr_1_1
Shorter version: **shorturl.at/jlpDX**

Sweet Love Letters to Jesus (Spanish language)

https://www.amazon.com/Cartas-Dulce-Amor-Jesus-intimidad/dp/168411862X/ref=tmm_pap_swatch_0
Shorter version: **shorturl.at/iovOZ**

References

[1] https://jewishjournal.com/ culture/217909/hebrew-word-week-navi-prophet/)

[2] https://www.abari,-publications.com/Meaning/Shechem.html#XrF3wxNKgW8

[3] "God's Prophetic Symbolism In Everyday Life, by Adam F. Thompson and Adrian Beale, © 2017, page 271

[4] https://www.abarim-publications.com/Meaning/Moreh.html#XrFrmRNKgW8)

[5] https://www.abarim-publications.com/Meaning/Moreh.html#XrFrmRNKgW8)

[6] https://ssnet.org/blog/early- and-latter-rain/

[7] https://www.abarim-publications.com/Meaning/Mamre.html#.X2ELnmdKgW8

[8] https://www.abarim-publications.com/Meaning/Shaveh.html#.X2ENY2dKgW8

[9] https:// www.abarim-publications.com/Meaning/Lot.html#.X2EOLWdKgW8

[10] https://overviewbible.com/melchizedek-facts

[11] "Numbers that preach" by Troy A. Brewer, © 2016, pgs. 139-145

[12] https://www.weekly. israelbiblecenter.com/the-meaning-of-the-hebrew-names/

[13] TPT Genesis 17:10 footnoted

[14] "Numbers that preach", by Troy A. Brewer, © 2016, pgs 94-105

[15] https://www.abarim-publications.com/Meaning/Isaac.html#.X2EXeWdKgW8

[16] https:// abarim-publications.com/Meaning/Mamre.html#Xr6YmBNKgW8

[17] Genesis 18:3 TPT footnote f

[18] "Numbers that Preach" by Troy A. Brewer, © 2016, pg 177

[19] "Numbers that Preach" by Troy A. Brewer, © 2016, pg. 160-162

[20] "Numbers that Preach", by Troy A. Brewer, © 2016, pgs. 59-70

[21] https://www.abarim-publications.com/Meaning/Isaac.html#.X2EXeWdKgW8

[22] https://www.abarim-publications.com/Meaning/Isaac.html#.X2EXeWdKgW8

[23] https://m.youtube.com/ watch?v=9uTXz9VHLXw

[24] Genesis 22:5 TPT – footnote e

[25] Genesis 22:2 TPT– footnote b

[26] Genesis 22:5 TPT – footnote e

[27] https://m.youtube.com/watch?v=9uTXz9VHLXw

[28] https://m.youtube.com/watch?v=9uTXz9VHLXw

[29] Genesis 11:28 TPT – footnote c

[30] Genesis 11:4 TPT – footnote o

[31] Genesis 12:1 TPT – footnote a

[32] https://www. abarim-publications.com/Meaning/Lot.html#.X2EdlmdKgW8

[33] Genesis 13:10 TPT – footnote a

[34] https:// thingsofthesort.com/bible-studies/2019/2/5/genesis-14-abram-rescues-lot- and-is-blessed-by-melchizedek

[35] https://www.jesuswalk.com/abraham

[36] Beva Metzia 87a

[37] Genesis 20:2 TPT – footnote d

[38] Genesis 16:2 TPT – footnote b

[39] Genesis 16:1 TPT footnote a

[40] "Looking Up" by Troy A. Brewer

[41] Genesis 15:17 TPT – footnote j

[42] James 2:23 TPT – footnote b

[43] Genesis 1:3 TPT – footnote a

[44] "God's Prophetic Symbolism In Everyday Life – Thompson, Beale – pg. 357

[45] "Numbers that Preach – Brewer – pg. 116

[46] https://www.mazzaroth.com/ Chapter Four/AbramsTransformationToAbraham.html

[47] Genesis 17:1 TPT – footnote f

[48] "The Alpha and the Omega" – Ch 4 – Jim A. Cornwell

[49] https://www.weekly.israelbiblecenter.com/ the-meaning-of-the-hebrew-names/

[50] Isaiah 9:6 TPT – footnote c

[51] https://www.chabad.org/ parshah/article_cdo/aid/1144592/jewish/What-did-Adam-Name-the- Animals.htp

[52] https://waynestiles.com/god-will-give-you-a-new-name/

[53] Revelation 2:17 TPT – footnote a

[54] Genesis 1:28 TPT – footnote g

[55] Kenneth Copeland, "The Blessing Of The Lord", pg. 27

[56] Strong's Concordance, 4406

[57] Genesis 24:67 TPT – footnote e

[58] Genesis 25:11 TPT – footnote b

[59] Genesis 49:1 TPT – footnote b

[60] Genesis 49:9 TPT – footnote a

[61] Dreams & Mysteries – The Mystery of the Father's Blessing: John Paul Jackson: https://youtu.be/D1GdgDw7H8g

[62] www.merriam-Webster.com/dictionary/Hall of Fame

[63] "Becoming A Hall of Famer" – website of Pro Football Hall of Fame

[64] www.savingcountrymusic.com/how-are-performers-elected-to-the-country-music-hall-of-fame/

[65] "The Complete Guide to the Bible", Stephen M. Miller, pg. 460

[66] TPT – Hebrews – Introduction

[67] Strong's H530

[68] www.bible.com/reading-plans/2487-7-hebrew-words-every-christian-should-know/day/2

[69] www.ancient-Hebrew.org/definition/faith.htm

[70] "Contemplations On Character" by Brian Guerin, pgs 52-53